CALL ME DIRECTOR

CALL ME DIRECTOR

Memoir of a Police Reformer

E. Winslow Chapman
and David Wayne Brown

SARTORIS
LITERARY
GROUP

ISBN: 979-8-9893644-0-4(HC)
Cover design: Sartoris Literary
Back Cover Photo: Haley Kirksey Graham

SARTORIS LITERARY GROUP
Metro-Jackson, Mississippi
SARTORISLITERARY [DOT} com

We dedicate this book to the many fine men and women in blue who work tirelessly and with integrity to protect and serve the people of Memphis and Shelby County, Tennessee, as well as to those who take a stand when police force reform is required.

E. Winslow Chapman

David Wayne Brown

CONTENTS

FOREWORD

I spent nearly 46 years as a copy clerk, reporter, editor, columnist, and editorial writer at *The Commercial Appeal* newspaper. Occasionally, someone will ask me what I feel was the most important story I covered.

My answer usually disappoints.

When you work for your hometown newspaper for more than four and one-half decades, frankly, it is hard to pick that "one" story. You remember sights, sounds and what people say.

There is one incident I remember that, for me, crystalized one of the crucial goals then-Memphis police Director E. Winslow (Buddy) Chapman wanted to accomplish when he took the helm of the Police Department in 1976—to gain the trust of the city's African-American citizens.

I was *The Commercial Appeal's* chief police reporter. I started that beat a month or two after the police strike in 1978. I stayed on the police beat until December 1982.

In 1977 and 1978, the U.S. Department of Justice began a review of the number of incidents in which police officers shot unarmed suspects or shot at suspects but missed. I remember one of the DOJ investigators telling me that it was a good thing Memphis police officers were bad shots.

Memphis African-American leaders and residents were understandably/rightly angry about the shootings since most of those who got shot were Black men. Each shooting brought a storm of protest. Yet they kept occurring.

One such shooting occurred in 1979 and I was prepared to report on the expected backlash. But, for the most part, there was no backlash.

A few days after the shooting, I was walking out of the main entrance of the police station when I ran into the late Herman Ewing, the long-time executive director of the Memphis Urban League. I asked him why African-American leaders were relatively quiet about the slaying.

Ewing told me the leaders, based on Chapman's efforts to curb police shootings and police brutality, were giving the director some grace to see how he would handle the situation.

Chapman fired the officer.

Because of Chapman's pledge to make himself open to the press, I had a front-row seat to many of the events described in this book. I was privy to the external and internal goings-on as the Director, among other things, also moved to improve training, better psychologically screen potential recruits, reduce police brutality incidents and shootings, make promotions more merit-based rather than good-old-boy based, and increase the number of Blacks and women in the Police Department.

It is my belief that Chapman wanted to make these changes during his tenure and the DOJ's involvement gave him the added muscle needed to break through the long-standing cultural barriers.

Perhaps more important are the gains he made establishing credibility within the Memphis African-American community.

Chapman did not just talk about change, he moved to change a decades-long police culture, a change that would not only benefit the African-American community, but the entire city.

If I could compare Chapman to a major-league baseball player, he occasionally struck out. However, his batting average was good enough to earn him a multi-year nine-figure contract. He was an outsider determined to modernize an entrenched bureaucracy. For the most part, he succeeded.

He was the right man in the right place at the right time.

— Jerome Wright

Abandoned Memphis police headquarters awaiting rescue.

Prologue

The neo-classical metropolitan police building in downtown Memphis — still imposing in its faded and neglected glory of marble and granite — was toiling through its final years of service.

The main first story room inside the Memphis Central Police Station clacked and rang one particular morning in 1977 with the usual sounds of police work: phones, typewriters, chatter. Cigarette smoke filled the air. Desks, chairs and members of the force were crammed along both sides of a central aisle.

No one looked up toward the long-forgotten rotunda, its splendor diminished by cracks, peeling paint and haphazard attempts to keep its craftsmanship intact. The portraits of past police chiefs looked on from the walls, their stares seeming to mingle with the ghostly memories of countless sergeants, detectives, inspectors, captains and deputy chiefs.

The four-story building was constructed in 1911. It and the fire station next door had been commissioned by future mayor E. H. Crump, then the commissioner of fire and police and not yet known as "Boss." It was a modernizing time in Memphis. The previous year Memphis had moved to a commission form of government and instituted civil service for government employees. The new police headquarters even had telephone and telegraph services.

Now it was 66 years later and the city was clawing its way out of a global recession followed by stagnation, and had no funds to renovate the crumbling interior. By 1982 the building would be shuttered and face decades of silent deterioration.

In the back of the building this day, however, a bit of police drama was about to unfold.

Behind the main room's rear wall, a short corridor connected the office of the Memphis Police Chief with that of the Memphis Police Director. Forty-four feet separated two men who for months had been in a partly private but at times public last-man-standing battle royale.

One man was chief. One man was director.

One would have to give way, for only one truly could be in charge of the Memphis Police Department.

William Oren (Bill) Crumby Jr. was an old-school cop who believed in toughness in all things. He sported a sizable ego to match his waistline. He wanted none of the reforms and outside viewpoints many in the community clamored for by 1977 and which were his opponent's daily motivation for work. Crumby was tired of "outside influence" and "outside agitators."

Crumby marched the short distance to Director E. Winslow (Buddy) Chapman's office. The chief was wearing his blue uniform and carrying a black briefcase. He had outlasted other insurgents and now had his sights on a new intruder from outside the department.

Director Chapman did not come up through the police ranks. Although he had ample police experience and knowledge, he was the city's first, and as of the third decade of the 21st century, only purely civilian head of police in Memphis.

Both men were born and raised in the city. Both were military veterans. Both were sure of the correctness of their positions. Each thought he had the ear and support of the majority of police personnel and, more important, of Mayor Wyeth Chandler himself.

Chapman was dressed in his usual starched shirt and tie. He stood up as Crumby gave a short greeting and then slapped the briefcase onto the desk.

The battle was about to move from trench warfare among police brass and politicos to a very personal, face-to-face encounter. The only question: who would be the first to blink?

Crumby got straight to the point. He announced he had ordered the "intelligence squad" to conduct an investigation on Chapman. He tapped the briefcase with his hand.

Either resign "like Hubbard did," said Crumby, "or I'll show what's in that briefcase to the newspapers, the city council and the mayor."

Director Chapman, taken by surprise and yet bemused, looked from the briefcase to Crumby's face.

"Tell you what, Chief. I'll be glad to provide you some transportation," he said.

The chief's face reddened.

Then he grabbed the briefcase and stormed from the room.

E. Winslow (Buddy) Chapman
Photo courtesy Special Collections Department,
University of Memphis Libraries

1

Face-off

The year 1968 struck Memphis like an earthquake.

The biggest tremors came in the wake of the city's sanitation strike and the assassination of Martin Luther King Jr. Rev. King gave his Mountaintop speech, was murdered, and Memphis fell into a deep valley of collective shame and financial withdrawal. The reverberations were to last for years and are ongoing.

The winter of 1968 also happened to be when the City of Memphis dropped the old commission form of government that had stood since 1910 and adopted a mayor-council form of government. The motivation for the change had been coming for 20 or more years. Citizens felt they didn't have true representation. Before the shift, the mayor and five elected commissioners managed the city and operated both as legislative and executive branches. The mayor had slightly more power than the other five, mainly through political maneuvering and the bully pulpit.

It was impossible in those days for any black citizen to win a race for mayor or commissioner. Even the great awakening to civil rights couldn't budge a barnacled power structure.

White citizens also were beginning to clamor for change. The question of consolidated city and county governments was put to voters in 1962. It failed, as it would in subsequent referenda. But the need to modernize the city's government with separate executive and legislative roles was clear. In 1966 voters agreed to the change in the City Charter (county government would follow suit a few years later). The new system would take place on the first day of January, 1968.

The change to mayor-council form greatly enhanced the power of the mayor. The title of all heads of major divisions of government switched from commissioner to director, and that is important to our story.

*****

Police departments are, and always have been, inherently political. They are influenced by the dominant political forces in the jurisdictions they serve, and internally by the power structure within, and often by the union if one exists.

I know. I had been in charge of an Army police force in occupied Germany and worked closely with various municipal forces. I had studied policing in college. I knew how hide-bound and insular a police department could be. I also knew how effective and responsive one could be with positive leadership. The Memphis Police Department (MPD) was mostly the former before I became its leader.

In the mid-twentieth century, the department often acted as a political campaign organization. Long-time *Memphis Press-Scimitar* reporter Menno Duerkson wrote about this at the end of his career.

"The Memphis Police Department was not only politically dominated, it was a political organization in July 1951," he wrote 27 years later.[1]

"Police officers did their political chores, on or off the job, without question," he continued. His comments came in a two-part series as he retired after 27 years reporting on the police.

---

[1] Memphis Press Scimitar, July 31, 1978

"They distributed poll tax receipts — to the right people. They rounded up voters, attended political rallies and acted as political couriers. On election days a political command post was set up right in the police headquarters building."

Starting in 1951, the man in charge of the MPD was Claude Armour. He was the only person to have held every single rank within the police department, thanks to the tremendous political power of his family in rural Shelby County. Armour had risen from patrolman to commissioner of fire and police in only five years. He was voted back into the office repeatedly with big majorities.

The Department also had the appointed position of chief of police and in 1951 that was Ed Reeves. But he knew that Armour was the undisputed "boss" of the department. When the position of Shelby County Sheriff opened in 1954, Reeves was "given" the candidacy and practically guaranteed election. One of his assistant chiefs, J.C. Macdonald, was moved to the job of chief.

Such political machinations were normal.

Macdonald would remain chief until 1968. He flourished in the political system and ran the department in the same fashion as his predecessor. He also had a reputation among policemen for being tough, honest and fair.

During that time the size of the MPD was growing rapidly. In 1951 the department had about 300 men, all white. By 1968 there were more than 1,000 officers, and there were fewer than 50 black patrolmen who were given limited assignments.[2]

When Macdonald took a job with the State of Tennessee, Assistant Chief Henry Lux became Chief Lux. Retired FBI agent Frank Holloman won the new position of director of fire and

---

[2] Memphis Press Scimitar, July 31, 1978

police. With the change in government, the power that Armour had enjoyed was diminished. Holloman stayed on the job a short time. When he retired again, the position was divided into two directorships, one of police and one of fire.

When I look back all these years later on my career in City Hall and as the city's police director, I can see that this came at a pivotal moment. The stage was set for new management in the mayor's office and in the police department. But the old system had to die out first.

It would go out with a roar.

Lux, who had inherited the position of chief, proved to be something of a reformer of police management and he began trying to dismantle the department's "good ol' boy" system. When he became chief he realized he had never had any actual management experience or education. He found in a desk drawer a 1963 study for Memphis by the International Association of Chiefs of Police — a detailed study he had never seen even as an assistant chief. He read through the report and started seeing what was wrong with the MPD's top-heavy structure.

At that time 34 percent of the police held ranks above patrolman. Experts had determined the number of command officers should be more like 10 percent. Because he was barred by local civil service rules from firing or demoting so many with higher ranks, Lux decided to freeze all promotions and he began assigning some top commanders to menial desk jobs. That angered many among the detectives and those ranked higher. In the lower ranks, since he couldn't offer promotions, he started a system of pay hikes and began to offer training in order to move toward more professionalism.

One thing Lux could not do was give all personnel what they

felt was proper representation and attention to their needs, and so the movement toward establishing a police union got under way.

Lux's career as the head of the police department will forever be defined in large part by the fact he led the department during the city's sanitation workers' strike that brought Dr. King to Memphis. There can never be a tougher job than to lead a police force that must monitor yet try to stay clear of thousands of people marching intensely and in some cases angrily for change, for fair treatment and for dignity.

Much has been written about the abused sanitation workers and events that led to violence in the march, then King's slaying and the aftermath with National Guard troops patrolling Memphis and riots across the nation. Some cities fared worse than ours.

For our purposes, let us remember that Lux worked for Mayor Henry Loeb. Loeb was undoubtedly racist. He lived and breathed law and order, with emphasis on *his* order. He hated attempts to unionize and he was uber-stubborn, to a major fault. He had an all-white cabinet of advisers who weren't able to steer him away from the crisis.

Lux tried to get his police force ready for what might come. Although without some of the equipment he needed and without proper rank-and-file training in massive crowd control, the Memphis Police were out in force that fateful spring day.

The best telling of all the events leading up to the march and all that happened later, in my opinion, can be found in the book *At The River I Stand: Memphis, The 1968 Strike, and Martin Luther King* by Joan Turner Beifuss. She wrote, in part, of the night of the assassination:

The police were caught in a frightful situation during the first hour after Dr. King's death as the trouble mounted. All available manpower was needed in the hunt for the murderer, and the false reports over a civilian radio band of the chase of a white Mustang, supposedly connected with the shooting, across the northern part of the city shortly after 6:30 p.m. had shaken up everyone at headquarters...

If heavy rioting were to begin in the black community — and police officers were convinced it would — the only way of stopping it would be to throw in massive forces at the outset. But there would be no massive forces until the National Guard could be moved onto the streets. And if any black violence turned against whites, would whites retaliate? Even men who would never think of using guns except on hunting trips into the dry stubby fields were glad the guns were there, in cases, on racks, in closets. Police knew the quick disposition of the National Guard would be as important in convincing some whites that they did not have to turn vigilante, that law enforcement forces were in control, as it would be in keeping actual order in the black neighborhoods, although the real fate of Memphis depended on which way the black community would go as the news that Dr. King was indeed dead shuddered across it.

As the night wore on, she and others reported, there were plenty of isolated incidents across the city. Fires were started and stores were looted. Rocks were thrown at police cars. Snipers took a few potshots. Overall, cooler heads soon prevailed in Memphis to the entire city's credit, but especially to the credit of the black community. This is not to paint over the dark times or the suffering. There was deep dismay and anger, smothered in grief, and yet a steadfast and long-practiced patience that allowed people to listen to black leaders calling for peace as King had preached.

The city was wounded and its black population hurt — would go on hurting — for a long time.

As Joan Beifuss wrote of the assassination: *...it was as if the gun had been turned on all of them.*

Once Lux started down the road to reform he saw other moves he wanted to make. But when it came time for a mayoral election, politically-minded, high-ranking officers worked tirelessly against him. The old police political system was still alive.

Wyeth Chandler was a young and ambitious city councilman at the time. He was destined to win election as mayor and was determined to have a new chief when elected. Chandler, an attorney, was fascinated with police work and liked to be around law officers. I had dipped into politics myself and had a keen interest in policing and police leadership. Our interests would somehow meet and meld in the months and years to come.

Lux could see that his fortunes had changed and decided to resign soon after Chandler's election. Ranking officers who wanted a return to the former command system had Chandler's ear and recommended Bill Price for the job. Price was an old-style policeman.

Chandler also needed a director of police. He chose a retired Marine brigadier general, Jay W. Hubbard, a military man in outlook and manner. This appointment would bring about a few changes for the better but more for the worse in the months to come.

Chandler had volunteered for and served a short time in the U.S. Marine Corps. He had great pride in that service. He learned about Hubbard from a fellow attorney who was active in the local Marines Reserve Unit. I thought the appointment was a problem, however. I was Chandler's new executive assistant by then and gave him my opinion that policemen are not Marines. The Mayor went ahead with the appointment anyway and it was confirmed by the city council.

Hubbard made one good move early on, which was to bypass Chief Price in the command structure and then find a way to ease him out of the department for a job elsewhere in city government. Hubbard effectively became fully in charge of the department, but the next chief would soon go to war against that fact.

His name was Bill Crumby and he was the biggest throwback to an earlier time of all those among the police brass.

Hubbard had little time to contemplate any steps Crumby might be taking to gather his forces. From the start the general was seen as a penultimate outsider, and his penchant for issuing snap orders just like a Marine officer was resented up and down the police ranks.

Just days into the job as director of police, Hubbard announced that salaries were not a priority as officers were "relatively well-paid." Not true. On average, bus drivers were better paid. Officers from patrolmen to assistant chiefs were outraged. Before that issue died down, a series of scandals hit the department including the revelation that scores of policemen were enjoying the attentions of a certain prostitute. Hubbard announced that in the future any officer accused of wrong-doing or abuse of a citizen would be required to take a lie-detector test, or be fired for refusing to do so.

Numerous clashes began occurring with ranking officers, and Mayor Chandler, who had wanted to be more involved in police operations and decisions, often found he was uncomfortably in the middle of the fights. Soon the biggest conflict was between Hubbard and Crumby. The Chief was just as militant in his own way as Hubbard and he was single-mindedly determined to restore power to the chief's position.

As the battle grew in intensity, Hubbard suddenly resigned to everyone's shock. No one saw it coming. Rumors soon circulated in the MPD and in city hall about the reason for his sudden departure.

As Otis Sanford reported in his book *From Boss Crump to King Willie: How Race Changed Memphis Politics*, "The salacious story ... was that Hubbard was surreptitiously caught with a prostitute and Crumby had obtained revealing pictures of the encounter."

Whether true or not, whether some kind of illicit sting operation led by Crumby had occurred, there certainly was a personal confrontation and as a result Hubbard decided to leave office and leave town immediately.

Crumby started that next day in 1974 in a festive mood. He gathered the brass around him and made plans to restore his position as the one in direct charge of police operations. There was plenty of backslapping and joking. But Crumby's failure to cooperate in any way with Director Hubbard wasn't lost on the Mayor, or on Chandler's chief administrative officer, Henry Evans. They began to consider my own request to be the police director.

It was after the election and before he took office that I first told Chandler I wanted to be considered for the position. I felt my experience in policing matched my interest. Now they both began to look at my tenure as executive assistant to the mayor and to consider the strong relationships I had developed with the wider community in that role.

It wouldn't be an easy decision for Chandler, though.

As a holdover from the previous form of government, the position of chief of police still existed and was a protected civil service position. Chandler and Crumby had known each other for years. They had been in school together and had maintained a personal relationship since that time. Even as Crumby moved to strengthen the chief's position in relation to director, he also pressed Chandler to be named director himself. Chandler, however, had doubts and knew it would be difficult to get a confirmation from city council members who knew Crumby's background and reputation.

Crumby, always looking for ways to gather intelligence, assigned two of his most loyal officers to be Chandler's bodyguards.

Despite his doubts, Chandler still named Crumby "acting director." Crumby now had almost everything he wanted and felt he would get the position permanently. Then destiny took a hand.

An irregular transfer of police funds to finance a police pistol team came to light. That mistake — and several public speeches Crumby made that were not to Chandler's liking — rang the bell on Crumby's plans: Chandler considered appointing me director after all. He was in no hurry to do so, however. For his part, Crumby, angry and hurt, wasn't going to abandon his plans so easily.

Almost immediately after Chandler's announcement that someone else would become police director, and before I had a chance to think about a new assignment, a campaign of negative rumors about me began circulating — a "volume of vindictive verbal viciousness unmatched in police department history," said an alliterative article in *The Commercial Appeal* in September, 1976.[3]

It began with the "revelation" that I had brought an illegal truckload of Coors beer — a brand not then available locally — into the city from Colorado. I had not done that, but I *had* purchased a case of Coors now and then from a guy I knew. This same man was arrested one day, just after crossing the bridge from Arkansas in a truck marked that it was carrying shrimp. Instead of shrimp he had a truckload of beer. He was pulled over, arrested and transported to police headquarters. Crumby called a reporter that day and said I was behind transporting the goods.

I wish I could've been in the room when the man apparently was persuaded to finger me as the godfather. I admit I did have a taste for Coors beer now and then. That was true for a lot of Memphians.

The facts were these: I had agreed to help the man whom I had known since childhood by renting a truck since he had lost his own truck in an earlier arrest for transportation of Coors. You could call me perhaps hoodwinked. The man told me he had a job bringing shrimp to Memphis from New Orleans, so I made arrangements for him through Hertz. I realized later he hadn't really mended his smuggling ways.

The incident won me the first of numerous editorial cartoon depictions in the newspaper. A Bill Garner drawing showed me in a car run over by a shrimp truck, a mountain of Coors beer cans spilling out on the front of my vehicle. It's one of my all-time favorite cartoons.

In a news story written by *The Commercial Appeal*'s Tom Jordan, the Mayor was reported to say my possession of untaxed

---

[3] Backdrop, The Commercial Appeal, September 5, 1976

beer — we could think of it now as "beergate" — would not affect my chances to become director of police.

"It must certainly be measured by the fact that Coors beer, for the purpose of consumption and not for resale, has been used by a multitude of people in Shelby County," Chandler said. "To my knowledge there has never been a prosecution by any law enforcement agency for such usage." He added, "It certainly would be measured by the fact that if he (Chapman) in this one instance used bad judgment, he has in the last five years used outstanding judgment 12 hours a day, week after week and year after year."[4]

I was still in the running for director. So was a local FBI agent named Holloway Cromer Jr. and one or two others but the handwriting on the wall spelled my name.

Shortly after Chandler announced his intention to appoint me to the directorship, he summoned me to his office. I was briefed on a crisis that was emerging. Unknown to anyone outside the police department there existed a "Domestic Intelligence Unit." Essentially it spied on citizens police brass were worried about. The unit had been formed during the 1960s and was especially active during the period leading up to King's assassination. It would ebb and flow depending on circumstances and police chiefs. But who were these citizens and under whose authority was information being collected now?

A student at Memphis State who had come home as a disillusioned soldier from Viet Nam and spoke up about it had discovered that police had a file on him. He filed a discovery suit in federal court to see the file. The police promptly destroyed the file. Not wanting me to be involved before even starting a new job,

---

[4] The Commercial Appeal, September 7, 1976

Chandler told me he had ordered the unit disbanded and all remaining intelligence files destroyed.

Chandler gave that task to his new assistant, a man named Richard (Dick) Hackett, who would become mayor a decade later. Hackett collected all the files and took them to an incinerator.

The incident showed another problem that existed in the police force. The intelligence collection on members of the public would return decades later, again becoming a black eye for the department in the 21st century. Bad habits are very hard to break.[5]

With that matter put aside, I was appointed director and approved a week later by the city council. I was 37 years old.

I knew there were many problems to solve in front of me, but I had to focus on Bill Crumby and his schemes an awful lot in the weeks ahead. One of the first tasks I had to do as director was to quash an elaborate command structure diagram Crumby had drawn. The reorganization, of course, put the chief's position in charge of all operations, and turned the director into a kind of liaison position between the MPD and city hall on budget and administrative matters only.

Now the battle was on in earnest between a new civilian in charge of the police (myself) and an old boys network police chief with the high goal of preventing me from taking charge. The fight would go on for months. It was bitter, often public, and gave the Mayor major headaches.

The newspapers kept score, commented in editorials that usually were on target, and published more hilarious cartoons. Like a tense chess match, Crumby and I moved our pieces around the

---

[5] On October 27, 2018 U.S. Judge Jon McCalla issued a ruling that the police department had violated a 1978 consent decree by spying on political activists. His decision came after a trial revealed the MPD conducted extensive surveillance of individuals and organizations through a fake Facebook profile.

board, captured pawns and rooks, watched for opportunities to put each other in check. At one point, Crumby announced he was quitting, then changed his mind.

Just about every move was reported and commented on. (What a difference between then and now. A newspaper's editorial was read by many people and had great influence on how people thought and acted. Editorial cartoons lampooned and sometime figuratively harpooned a person, idea or plan. I miss the daily strong voice of the press in local community affairs.)

Once in December, 1976 Crumby issued what he called a "Command Bulletin." It said he was taking over all command and staff functions. I advised him in response that as appointed head of the MPD, all orders, memoranda, bulletins, letters or press releases had to be cleared through me.

Check but not checkmate.

People wondered why Chandler allowed the duel to go on for as long as it did. One particular conversation I had with the Mayor helped me better understand the ongoing predicament, and Chandler's outlook.

"You have to get along with Chief Crumby," he ordered.

"Mayor, I try to get along with all my subordinates."

I remember him looking at me in puzzlement, and then a kind of dawning realization passed across his face: that Crumby was in fact subordinate to me. That was the very point of view Crumby did not want Chandler to have.

All along, I was taking small steps toward my own ideas for police department reforms. Not only did I see the need for reform and want to make changes, but under three looming U.S. judicial consent decrees, there was no choice but to act if the city didn't want to see a federal takeover of the entire police department.

In October 1977 I had said at a public hearing on police attitudes toward the community that my appointment would prove "earthshaking" and I vowed to assure that no one's civil rights would be violated.

The Tennessee Advisory Committee to the U.S. Commission on Civil Rights had come to Memphis for a two-day hearing at the Federal Office Building downtown. Looking back, I can see now that I was walking far out on a limb, so to speak.

"You cannot understand the literally earthshaking effect my appointment had on the (police) department," I assured the committee. "I am not a police officer. I have not been associated with the department in the past, and I have no associates in the department.

"This will force the department to take an entirely new look at where they're going, because they have to decide where I'm going, and I'm the boss."

I was making a lot of pledges and doing so publicly. I was pushing a rock uphill. Did I know how heavy the rock was? Probably not.

Almost every day during my first months in office, festering problems in the police department were coming to the surface. These included the theft of unclaimed items guarded by police; the theft of undercover funds and that theft being ignored by a deputy chief; the abuse of police overtime funds, plus the fact that U.S. Law Enforcement Assistance Administration standards for use of federal funds weren't being met.

The stolen undercover funds implicated several in the command staff. Second only to Chief Crumby in rank and control was Deputy Chief George Hutchinson. He was acting chief in the absence of Crumby, who had taken an out-of-town trip.

Eli Arkin, who had been charged with the actual theft, was close to Crumby and Hutchinson. Captain Pat Ryan, the commander of the Intelligence Squad, had told Hutchinson the missing funds were sure to be uncovered due to an order I had made, in the wake of missing unclaimed items, that all cash funds were to be thoroughly accounted for.

Instead of reporting to me about the stolen undercover money, Hutchinson removed Ryan from his position and told Arkin to replace the funds and resign. It was a classic case of "business as usual." I called an administrative hearing to review the sequence of events, terminated Arkin and referred his case to the Shelby County Attorney General's office. I reduced Hutchinson in rank from deputy chief to inspector and moved him to an administrative position.

These steps, plus my appointment of the city's first black precinct commander, led to Crumby's short-lived announcement that he would leave. Two weeks later he said he would stay on until he was 60 years old. I attempted to ignore him and continued my efforts rooting out internal corruption and waste.

It was at this time that I was approached by a member of the department's command staff. He said his daughter was working in the city's Finance Division and was put in a difficult position because of a controversy between city and county governments over the purchase of a computer system.

I called the city's director of finance and learned that a police department employee named Gene Banton was the one involved. I had never heard of the employee or the organization he headed. I discovered that he had been an administrative sergeant who, with Chief Crumby's help, had been named director of something called the Metro Law Enforcement Planning Group. I then learned we were paying him an inspector's salary, out of grade for the position, and that his actual job was writing Crumby's correspondence.

When I learned that Sheriff Gene Barksdale also had concerns over the legitimacy of the position, I decided to reassign Banton to his previous position and conferred his duties on my own Deputy Chief of Administration Harris Cole. (Banton would later tell me he regretted getting caught up in Crumby's plots. He was a young man with a keen interest in law enforcement and the Chief took advantage of his enthusiasm.)

A furious Crumby announced he would use his own position with an organization called the Law Enforcement Coordinating Council (LECC) to reverse my decision. This was another group I'd never heard of. I was beginning to wonder how many there were. I soon discovered that the LECC was made up of the mayors and police chiefs from Bartlett, Collierville, Germantown, Memphis and Millington, as well as representatives from City Council, Shelby County's Quarterly Court, and other Mid-South governing bodies. Its purpose was to seek funding grants and divvy up the result.

When I let Crumby know that I would be replacing him on the coordinating council, he demanded that Mayor Chandler determine whether I had the authority to do that.

I felt now we were coming to some kind of a conclusion about who was to be in charge of the Memphis Police Department. Mayor Chandler found himself in a position where he no longer could ignore the question of authority. He walked to the Central Police Headquarters Building and found his way to my office. Crumby joined us.

Chandler heard us out and then issued a statement that the police director was the correct representative to the LECC. He told the newspapers that the fight for control of the police had calmed. But only six days later Crumby issued the command bulletin naming himself in control of all but budget and lesser administrative matters.

All the while more troubles were revealed. A federal grand jury issued 50 subpoenas to police officers under investigation for accepting favors from topless clubs in the city. This wasn't the first time that police personnel participation in illicit sex had been uncovered. Next an audit of overtime hours revealed that some officers had been granted authority to self-approve their own overtime payments.

I also learned that some driving while intoxicated case jackets had been unlawfully removed and destroyed, and that one intoxicated and injured prisoner had been dumped out of a squad car instead of being processed properly. These obviously were personal favors. Then a police lieutenant was charged with sexually assaulting two women.

I was busy putting out fires.

One day Crumby, again reneging on a promise to retire, filed an "appeal" to the Mayor's office and City Council, claiming total operational control of police and demanding that both agree to his claim. He said he would seek legal redress. He met with the Mayor. When he heard a detailed explanation by City Attorney Cliff Pierce about the responsibility of division directors under the new city charter, he said he would delay any "legal action."

Bluster doesn't always work.

Finally the day came when Crumby decided he had to force

me to leave office "like Hubbard did" and walked to my office to display the briefcase of files about me. He didn't take me up on the offer to drive him to the newspaper offices. He went there himself.

The next morning I was sipping from a cup of hot coffee when Wyeth Chandler called me on the phone.

"What in the *hell* is going on?" he said in that deep, gruff voice of his.

I told him about the briefcase containing "intelligence squad" information and reminded him that he had never believed the similar stories about what Crumby had done to Hubbard that made him leave town so quickly.

Chandler was as mad as I'd ever known him to be. He couldn't believe that Crumby would investigate me without consulting him or that he would feel free to make it public. He conferred with Evans and Pierce and then gave Crumby an ultimatum: resign or be fired, civil service guarantees be damned. Crumby's decision to retire came on February 2, 1977.

And what about that briefcase of uncovered intelligence on yours truly, E. Winslow (Buddy) Chapman?

I remember the day vividly. I had established a protocol with Crumby when I took charge. We were to address each other by our titles. His was Chief. "Call me Director," I had told him.

That morning I knew something was up when he came through the door and used my nickname.

"Good morning, *Buddy*."

Those files contained no evidence of wrongdoing. Most of Crumby's "information" proved false. But the news stories contained a couple of embarrassing financial points I did not enjoy reading about myself.[6]

---

[6] The Commercial Appeal, January 27, 1977

2

Plowboy to Plebe

Buddy Chapman distinctly recalls a sunny day in the 1950s. He was about to get into his beat-up old army Jeep when he heard a commotion of vehicles approaching the long drive up the hill to the family's home place called Goodwinslow.

As the teen-aged Chapman watched, a black limousine was approaching the house. In front were two escorting motorcycle patrolmen. Two more followed.

"What the ...?"

The entourage came to a halt on the gravel drive. In the vehicle's back seat sat Italy's ambassador to the United States. He had come to Nashville in the course of his duties and so was taking some extra days to drive to Memphis and visit his longtime friend, author and erstwhile world traveller, Mrs. Anne Goodwin Winslow.

Chapman politely bowed to the well-dressed gentleman who exited the vehicle, and led the way into the house for the reunion with his grandmother.

*****

As my background and the varied experiences of my upbringing shaped me in many ways — and I believe prepared me for police work — I'll provide an account of those years.

My father's ancestors came to West Tennessee on a rough-hewed log river craft. The raft held a small house for sleeping and a pen for livestock. The family floated the Tennessee River from North Carolina. That was in the early 1800s and they settled in wilderness. They built a log cabin near the Mississippi River and led a hardscrabble existence, farming north of today's Memphis.

When my father, Charles S. Chapman, grew up, he worked the fields and never went to school. He always said he'd visited two nearby states — north Mississippi and east Arkansas — and that was all he ever saw of the wider world.

My mother Mary was a 1929 graduate of Vassar College. She was the descendant of a John Winslow who came to the "New World" on the Mayflower and served as the second governor of the Plymouth Colony. That Winslow family remained a prominent factor in the Northeast. One antecedent, Admiral John Ancrum Winslow, is famous for sinking the Confederate warship *Alabama*, ending Admiral Raphael Semmes' reign of terror on Northern commerce at sea.

The admiral's grandson, Ebenezer Eveleth Winslow, later graduated first in his class at West Point and was given his choice of service branch and duty assignment. He chose the Army Corps of Engineers. Soon he was assigned to the newly created post of District Engineer of the Lower Mississippi River Valley, headquartered in Memphis.

After settling in Memphis, he one day took a ride by streetcar to a popular local resort at the Raleigh Springs where a large hotel had been built in 1892 at the site of several warm springs, and adjacent to where my grandmother Anne Goodwin lived. Her father, William W. Goodwin, came to the area in the 1860s from Nashville as a young law school graduate. He obtained a land grant and built a log cabin in Raleigh. When the Civil War began Goodwin joined the cavalry force formed by Nathan Bedford Forrest and rode with the general throughout the war. When he returned home he found his cabin had been burned and so he began a 12-year project to build a new home. That was where my grandmother was born.

It was while Ebenezer Winslow strolled the hotel's grounds that he met Anne Goodwin. After a proper courtship they married. Winslow's career in the Corps of Engineers later took them to far-flung places but they finally returned to the family home, which now was called Goodwinslow. (My grandmother authored several books, including one about the house called *The Dwelling Place*.)

Upon my grandfather's death, my mother inherited a large tract of farmland he had acquired in a remote northwest corner of Shelby County, Tennessee. She hired a man to operate the farm for her.

He soon had a working farm going. It produced most of the food requirements for the family and a sizable work force, and made a profit.

My mother subsequently married the overseer.

Until after the Second World War, cultivation was done with mule power. The farm had nearly 200 of them in those days. The biggest were used for logging. They would pull the logs from our sawmill to where a building or fence line was to be constructed. These mules could weigh as much as 1600 pounds. Each had a name.

Many families suffered during war rationing times, but my mother said the only items they had trouble getting were coffee and sugar. The farm raised beef and pork that was smoked and cured, vegetables for canning. We had milk and butter, made sorghum molasses. My father even had a way to sun-dry fruit with chicken wire swung horizontally between poles to allow the sun to do its work.

A few years later, my parents divorced and he settled on a

small farm in a nearby county. It was during my frequent parental visitations with him that I learned to harness a mule and plow the ground. I mainly used what was called a middle buster, and a walking cultivator. A middle buster plow, or a potato plow, is considered a plow that gently turns the earth. When you run the plow it drags a line along the middle of the path and you are left with a soft opening for planting seeds, tubers, bulbs and the like.

I now lived a life on two farms — one attached to the house in Raleigh and the other, my father's farm. Among my many farm duties, I milked the family cow every day from the age of six until I graduated from high school.

My father was older than my mother. He died in 1953 at the age of 65.

I look back on those days and find them far off and almost unbelievably idyllic.

We had a very good foreman on the farm in Raleigh but my mother expected me to gradually assume more and more responsibility. I lived a childhood of working and exploring nearly 1500 acres of woods and fields, horses and camping, swimming and sailing in a lake, and almost total freedom. Of course, all this came with the responsibility of cutting acres of grass, feeding livestock, milking, baling hay for winter, working the vegetable garden, cutting firewood, curing meat in a smokehouse, and building fires in winter for several large fireplaces in the house.

As I grew up, the Raleigh farm began to give way to subdivisions. The sale of lots had become the family's primary income by the middle of the 20th century. As the property gradually diminished in size, I took over its operation. Throughout high school, instead of participating in sports, I had special permission to leave school an hour early each day to work the farm with the remaining farmhands.

By the time I was 14 I had a restricted driver's license. My mother helped me buy a surplus Jeep. In the fall I would pull a loaded cotton trailer to a nearby gin in the morning and then pick up the empty trailer and a check for the bales after school, then pull the trailer home.

By the time I graduated from high school, I was the owner of two tractors, a hay baler, various other implements and the beat-up Jeep.

By the summer of 1956, after my grandmother had died, my mother announced I needed to experience Europe. I was 15 years old. The family house was closed. The latest cow, named Maryanne, went to a neighbor for milking and the horses and dogs moved to the care of other friends.

We took a train to New York and got passage on the *Exochorda*, a 475-foot vessel operated by the American Export Lines. She was a relatively small passenger cruiser, a freighter retrofitted for both freight and passengers, but seemed enormous to me. The ship had staterooms, a dining room, stage for shows and even a swimming pool.

We ate each night with officers and got to know the purser well. His name was Corey and he had a mynah bird which knew quite a few words, including "Where's Corey?" A new dance called the jitterbug was popular then. My older sister and I had taken dance lessons and were often called on to exhibit the dance in the evenings.

Our first stop in Europe was Barcelona, Spain, where the ship was to unload cargo. I was fascinated with the procedure: one cable, two booms, two winches that worked together very efficiently. This farm boy was gaining a new education.

After the stop in Barcelona we sailed to Genoa, Italy. There was history behind that decision.

My grandfather — my mother's father — was a distinguished West Point graduate. He had been stationed in Honolulu to design and build the fortifications at Fort DeRussy on Waikiki Beach when my mother was born. Following that assignment he was ordered to the Panama Canal to build new fortifications there.

My grandmother refused to live in Panama's hot, humid and mosquito-rich environs and moved back to the family home in Raleigh. Then she decided to take a vacation to Italy, accompanied by her two children who were my mother and uncle.

This was just before the outbreak of hostilities that became World War I. Their return trip was booked out of Genoa for arrival 10 days later in New York City. However, the ship was requisitioned by the Italian government. My grandmother decided to get tickets on a southbound train and disembark in the first place that looked nice — a town with a nearby hotel on the water.

That town turned out to be Santa Margherita, on the bay at Porto Fino. The Contenantale Hotel there was owned by a Ciano family which today owns numerous high-end properties in Italy. The Cianos had two children, the ages of my mother and uncle, and they all became close friends. On subsequent family trips to Europe, Caesare and Tilde Ciano were grown-ups and running the hotel. We always were treated as family members.

On that first European trip, after a week in Santa Margherita, we sailed up the coast toward Naples. We were headed to the Isle of Capri. Our ship — the *Andrea Doria*, longer and more luxurious than the *Exochorda* — was scheduled to pick up passengers in Naples and then head to New York. We said goodbye to the people we met on our short voyage. Days later the *Andrea Doria* was 300 miles east of New York on its transatlantic trip when it collided with a Swedish ship at night and in fog, and went down. Most passengers were rescued but 51 died.

We took a hydrofoil to Capri and stayed at a cliff hotel overlooking the sea. I remember having my first slice of pizza there. We returned to Naples and then boarded a train to Rome. I had had American train rides, including a trip to Lake Placid to ski, but they were nothing like the fine accommodations aboard most European trains.

Of all the sights in Rome — including the Vatican, the catacombs and the Circus Maximus, which seemed too small to me for chariot races — I was most impressed by the statue of Moses by Michelangelo in the Church of San Pietro, and learning that he polished its marble with seaweed.

From Rome we headed north through the country's lakes and finally through the Alps. I saw Zermatt and the Matterhorn. I was viewing in person what I had seen only in photographs in books back at Goodwinslow.

As a young woman my mother almost became a Swiss citizen. I learned all about the episode. The whole family did.

When she graduated from Vassar — the very same day my uncle graduated from West Point — my mother soon was on her way to Lausanne to study at the International Language School in that city. She had shown considerable aptitude for languages in college. While in Switzerland she met and fell in love with a mountain guide named Rodolph. With his help she climbed most of the major peaks in Europe. We have family photos of her on top of Mont Blanc and The Eiger.

Before the wedding, however, Rodolph fell through a snow-covered crevasse atop a glacier. As is usually the case in such accidents, his body was never found.

For the rest of her life my mother kept in touch with his family, who resided in Bern. We visited them several times through the years. My sisters and I were always treated as part of that family. On my first trip they made arrangements for my sister and me to stay at a hotel in Heidelberg — by ourselves. I was 15 and she was 19. We were to go on later and meet mother in Paris. Suffice it to say I grew up a lot in Heidelberg.

If the Italian trains were nice, the Swiss trains were better and the German trains superb. We got overnight tickets to Paris on a Rapido, the high-speed trains at the time. In the middle of the night we crossed into France and awoke to find ourselves on a siding in the middle of a large cabbage field. Not so "rapido" once you got into France.

Paris, of course, was everything I expected, only more so. We did all the normal sightseeing. On our third night I wasn't sleepy and so took a stroll through the streets. That stroll became a walk into trouble.

I found a bar and some very nice young women kept bringing me drinks. It was when I was presented the bar bill that I knew I was in trouble. The police were summoned, my mother was phoned, and I was allowed to go home with her. She spoke perfect French and I sure did appreciate that talent for languages then.

We made our way to London, saw the city like the tourists we were, and I learned that one can eat well in England if one only orders breakfast three times a day.

We crossed the Atlantic for the return home aboard a Cunard Lines ship called the *Parthia*. It was grand but we encountered rough seas and most passengers were ill. I felt fine, though, and ate meals in a nearly empty dining room.

When we glimpsed the Statue of Liberty — always a moving experience — I deeply felt my freedom and in more ways than one.

*****

I was never a very good student in school. My grades were good enough but I was far from a top performer. Once I was finished at Bartlett High School, which was then a rural school, I began to consider college possibilities. I had not thought that much about it until then.

Even though five men from her family had attended either Annapolis or West Point (three went to the U.S. Naval Academy and two attended the U.S. Military Academy), my mother had never broached the subject with me.

I somehow awakened to the prospect of attending one that summer. She wasn't opposed to the idea. Her father and her brother both had attended West Point. I considered that, but I liked the idea of being a pilot and Navy Air appealed to me especially.

So we settled on seeking an appointment and preparing for the entrance exams.

The service academies each had their own testing systems at that time. Today there are standard tests. My mother learned of a pair of local women, sisters, who had a business helping young people prepare for the tests. But when they learned where I had gone to school they flatly said they couldn't possibly get me ready.

That day my mother decided she would get me ready herself.

She was only 18 when she graduated at the top of her Vassar class. She knew she could prepare me as well as anyone

I began daily classes in math, science and geography, with the aid of the many books in our home library. At one point in math class, after doing quite well, I lost my way in algebra. When she asked me what the problem seemed to be, I told her how my algebra teacher, a Mrs. Briggs, had broken her leg and the rest of the term we had substitute teachers and the learning came to a halt.

Through family and political connections — including the recommendation of Walter Chandler, a U.S. congressman and city mayor before his son, Wyeth, won election — I gained what was known as a principal appointment and was scheduled to take the examination in the early spring of 1957.

There were 18 other candidates. We went through three full days of testing in the basement of the main U.S. Post Office downtown that today is a law school. We mostly were tested in math and science and many of the problems and questions were complex.

Years later I mentioned to a classmate that I was amazed I had passed.

"Hell," he replied. I don't think I did!"

I reported to Annapolis in June. My aunt, who lived in Washington, D.C., met my plane and after a night's rest she put me on a bus to start the next phase of my life. At the Maryland Avenue Gate to the Naval Academy I entered and made the turn for the long walk to Bancroft Hall. I remember wondering what I had gotten myself into. I now realize I was so very young.

The transition from young civilian to midshipman is transformative in too many ways to count.

I was directed to a room with others. We undressed and we were told to put everything but our wristwatches in the bag we had brought with us. We filled out a shipping tag. My mother later said getting that bag was like receiving the belongings of someone who had passed away.

In a sense that was true.

We then got into a long line. There were about 1,600 of us. In that line we received every item we would need. What we didn't put on we put into a duffel bag we received in that line. A long summer of drills, classroom work, and standing at post commenced. A letter I wrote home said it all:

"They take away every right you have, and then give them back one by one as 'privileges.'"

By the end of "Plebe Summer" we had lost several hundred potential members of the Class of '61. For some reason I did well in the stress of that summer. I determined to stay through the constant physical and emotional demands. But the start of the academic year was another matter.

I had never seen a slide rule. Grading was on a bell curve and quite a few of my classmates had attended college courses. Soon I was teetering on the edge of dismissal due to academic performance, or lack thereof.

But the Academy really wants to keep those with a genuine desire to stay and there was an excellent set of extra instruction courses that I attended. Classes were always overlaid with demands and discipline. I have told many young people since that it is critical to be able to think about more than one thing at a time. You also must be absolutely sure you want to be in a service academy for the long haul because they are masters at convincing many recruits that they really don't want to complete the training.

I still sat near the bottom of the ranks, but I also continued to hold on. We lost more members (some by suicide because of the demands and subsequent stress).

In the end I prevailed. My mother came up for the Class of 1961's June Week. As tradition demands, we gathered enough class members to scramble up and place our caps atop the Herndon

46

Monument which had been duly greased by the class ahead of us.

I told my mother I would never again be a plebe for the rest of my life.

The year following Plebe was known as Youngster Year and it was better for me, even though there was a heavy load of coursework. My grades were improving incrementally and I started to catch up and even surpass some in my class.

That year I even learned analytical calculus, but couldn't understand how it and other forms of math could be used or useful in life.

My second class year was my most successful. Courses were even harder but all were interesting. I was catching my stride. I was rating high on military studies and I was usually close to the top in inspections.

I was tapped to wear stripes in the next year, confusingly known as First Class Year. The distinction was determined by appearance in inspections, military bearing and class standing.

Although I had previously passed the course in analytical calculus, I didn't really know what I would ever do with the skill. It seemed to me a manipulation of numbers to obtain an answer with no real meaning. But then I was chosen for a group who had shown promise in navigation and we were put in an experimental course on how to mathematically figure the probability of an event. We learned that by using analytical calculus, we could produce the result we needed. Now my old nemesis was making sense.

A highlight of that year occurred when our Company was picked to participate in John F. Kennedy's inauguration. When all military units formed, Ninth Company, USNA was directly in front of the podium. We had a front row view of history.

As graduation approached it was time to submit our Choice of

Duty assignments. They would be carried out based on our preferences, class standing and qualifications.

My choices were Surface Navy, Marine Corps, Army or Air Force. At that time in the Academies it was possible to accept a commission in a separate military branch. This was when 20/20 uncorrected vision was required and I no longer qualified for my early desire to go into Navy Air.

I strongly considered the Marines, but that would have meant an assignment at sea. I was scheduled to be married after graduation. When the U.S. Army offered assignment to an armored unit in West Germany, where my new wife could accompany me, I took the Cold War stationing.

The idea of living in Europe helped me make up my mind, so in 1961 I became a Second Lieutenant in the United States Army. I didn't know it then, but my life in the Army was to lead me down a path toward becoming the first civilian director of police in Memphis history.

3

Finding my calling

In 1962 the Cold War was closer to hot than most people realized. If a Soviet invasion were to happen in Western Europe, a military analysis pointed to the Fulda Gap where hostilities would begin against American occupying forces. This lowland corridor runs southwest from the German state of Thuringia to Frankfurt am Main and was considered the spear point where a war could start. The Fulda Gap happened to be the shortest and easiest route from the border between East and West Germany to the Rhine River. Both NATO and Warsaw Pact military forces stayed heavily concentrated in the area. Daily there were constant patrols, surveillance teams and alerts carried out on both sides of the border. Many observation points stood less than 100 yards apart.

The Fulda Gap was uneasy, restless and tense.

The Fulda Gap also was where a young lieutenant from Memphis assigned to the U.S. Army's 12th Cavalry found himself a year after graduating from the U.S. Naval Academy.

How he got there, and how that assignment ultimately led him down a path toward becoming director of the Memphis Police Department, is a dramatic part of our story.

*****

After attending Armor School at Fort Knox, Kentucky, and Airborne School at Fort Benning, Georgia, I received my first assignment as a platoon leader in the 12th Armored Cavalry Squadron in Budingen, Germany.

49

My orders took me first to Fort Dix, New Jersey, for transportation to Europe. After a very long flight I arrived in Frankfurt just before Christmas 1961. I was soon on the job.

The 12th Cavalry was detached from the main units of the Division and rotated along the border with another Cavalry unit. Our job was to serve as a trip wire should any incursion by the Soviets occur. The squadron consisted of four companies, plus support. Each company had four platoons, with each having four Scout Jeeps, two tanks, a mortar armored carrier and an infantry armored carrier. If needed, each company could be reconfigured quickly into all-tank or all-infantry platoons. We were a versatile and agile force.

Because the Army had been experiencing a shortage of company grade officers at the time, I was about to assume a position that had been filled temporarily by the platoon sergeant. I wondered how that was going to go. I learned that Sgt. Nance had joined the army at 17, fought in WWII and earned a battlefield commission, attaining the rank of major. Because of a drinking problem he had been reduced to staff sergeant.

As it turned out, I had nothing to be concerned about. I couldn't have had a more supportive and faithful sergeant. I lost count of how many times I heard him say, "Now Lieutenant, I recommend …" That always meant I was about to get the benefit of his vast experience.

Years later when he was forced to retire he moved to Memphis where, he said, he knew someone (me). He didn't last long in civilian life, dying soon after.

I also met in Germany a man who was the company com-mander's driver. J. R. Bramlett was from Pontotoc, Mississippi, and has been a life-long and treasured friend. Even on field day,

Bramlett always was ready for inspection and that included the captain's Jeep.

He and other drivers bunked in special quarters on the second floor above headquarters offices. I arrived one early morning to find three injured men lying on the ground near the office entrance. I investigated and learned that the three men had sneaked into Bramlett's room to beat him up to settle some score. He had thrown all three of them out his window.

Two days after my arrival a short exercise was scheduled for the squadron. Because I was so new, the commander decided that I would go only as an observer. Nance would remain in charge. I was assigned a Jeep and driver so I could get acclimated to the workings of the unit.

Army field maps rely on topographical features such as hills, streams and valleys. Road signs can be moved, changed or destroyed, so it is important to learn where you are by those maps. I had always been adept at maps and charts and so kept a watch on the progress. When we stopped to make camp, I approached the captain with a request. I told him of an interesting feature near the place that had been designated on the map by headquarters as our destination. Could I have permission to go look at it since I didn't have other duties?

"What do you mean? That's where we are," he replied.

I respectfully answered that actually we weren't where we were supposed to be and pointed out the correct location on the map. He quickly ordered everything reassembled and we moved to our assigned location.

I saved him from trouble for being in the wrong place, and I doomed myself to becoming the person appointed to find our correct position whenever we were in the field.

The squadron was scheduled for winter training at a former German camp — "Grafenwoehr " —outside Nuremburg, near the Czechoslovakian border. The winter brought the lowest temperatures and most snow of any winter since 1942. The Rhine River froze and the West German army was required to transport heating oil by tanker trucks on the Autobahn as an emergency measure.

We loaded equipment onto railroad flatcars and troops in passenger cars in a blinding snowstorm for the two-day trip. Our tanks had to be perfectly aligned on the beds because the outside edge of the tank's tracks extended almost a foot beyond the edge of the cars. A lot of tunnels were narrow, so railroad inspectors measured the width of vehicles closely.

The snow and ice made loading difficult and dangerous. More than once when loading and again when unloading a tank would nearly slip off the side of a car. Each time the tank would have to be "walked" off with one tread on the ground and one still on the rail car. It was slow going.

When we arrived at our destination our billets were old and poorly heated. That didn't matter much because most of our time was spent out in the field or on firing ranges. We experienced many unannounced alerts and rapid changes in deployment orders. This all was designed so that we could practice for action in real-world bad conditions.

We saw a lot of mine shafts in the countryside. They were easy to identify because columns of steam came out from their relative warm and moist interiors. One challenge we had was to prevent the men from going inside these mines to warm up. If they did that, the moisture would seep into their clothing and create the potential for frostbite once they got back outside.

Our proximity to the artillery range meant that we could clearly hear the rounds spinning over our heads. I was fascinated to find that you actually could detect the rounds rotating as they passed through the air above us.

At one point in this deployment the snow got so heavy that only the tanks could move through it. We looked like gypsy caravans, with each tank pulling two trucks and two or three Jeeps into positions. We had to keep the tanks running to make sure the diesel fuel didn't thicken and refuse to flow.

I was in Graf two more winters after that first time, but it never was as bitter as in January of 1962. When the time came I was very glad to return to our Kaserne[7] in Budingen.

On return we resumed our regular rotation duties as advance warning scouts. The border was irregular and the East German border guards, the infamous Grenzpolizei, often were confrontational and eager to create an incident. They probably were bored, but always watched for an opportunity to apprehend an individual or vehicle.[8]

This meant that any time we approached the border we always traveled in pairs, at least, so that one could remain in radio contact with the base. There were different radio codes for different scenarios.

I have often told people since that a gun fired *at* you sounds entirely different from hearing one shot into the distance. I was fired on more than once as a harassment technique. One incident

---

[7] Kaserne: A loanword taken from the German meaning "barracks". It is the typical term used when naming the garrison location for American and Canadian forces stationed in German.

[8] The *Grenztruppen*'s main role was preventing the illegal migration from the GDR (East Germany), and was controversially responsible for many deaths at the Berlin Wall. (*Wikipedia*)

involved a driver and myself and occurred one day during another heavy snowfall.

We had stopped in what seemed an uninhabited location and both got out of the vehicle to answer a call of nature. We got out each side of the Jeep and left the radio behind. It was a clear violation of orders. When I finished and turned back I was met with automatic weapon fire, the bullets hitting the snow in front of me. The same thing happened to the driver on his side. We both hit the ground. He stayed down, but when I started to rise, more bullets punctured the snow.

We were required to check in at certain intervals with a duty officer at company headquarters. I now was behind the appointed time. I heard the officer over the radio asking for a report on our situation. I tried to get up and again I saw the bullets spattering holes in the snow in front of me. Clearly we seemed to be pinned down. At this point the duty officer said if I didn't respond immediately he was required to call in a division alert. That in turn could result in a U.S. Army Europe alert and I didn't want to have to explain myself to that audience.

The idea of a court martial made me think over the situation clearly and quickly. I decided that if the sharpshooter had wanted to hit me he would have. I stood up slowly and walked to the Jeep, praying the sniper had good aim. Gunfire erupted but the bullets stayed several feet in front of me.

I grabbed the radio mike and, as calmly as I could, answered the call from headquarters, feeling grateful that whoever was on the other side of the border didn't have bad aim.

During my time in Germany I had the sense I was performing a very small part of a very big drama.

When we were off border patrol and back in the garrison, we

did constant training and field drills. That included periodic training alerts that almost always came in the middle of the night and sometimes involved several days and movements in response to orders.

I one day was detached to division headquarters in Frankfurt to assume the role of a rank several above my own for practice of various scenarios. One involved my taking the role of a night duty officer at the regimental level in a combat situation. I had a list of resources at my disposal and could use them — only on paper, of course.

In the exercise I was told that a critical supply depot was under attack by a force of insurgents and civilians. I responded by sending a company of military police to restore order. I then was advised that the MPs had been overwhelmed and the attacking force had grown in size.

I looked through my resource list and at the bottom I found an armored cavalry squadron that was said to be in a refit mode but available to respond. I decided to skip steps and detach the squadron to the scene. The exercise suddenly was stopped and I found myself facing a brigadier general and two colonels.

What had prompted me to jump so far down my list of resources and increase the size of my force to that extent, the general demanded?

I said if the company of MPs had been overwhelmed and the insurgent force was growing, slowly and incrementally increasing our response might not be effective. I knew the attack had to be stopped and that that could be done immediately by sending a full cavalry squadron.

The general grunted. I was rewarded a commendation for making a good decision.

It was around this time that fate truly stepped forward in my life and with lasting consequences.

One thing I definitely had never thought about was doing police work. We shared our Kaserne with an artillery unit. We were detached from the division at a remote base and so didn't have the usual military police presence for security. We instead had a Unit Police. It was a rotating assignment with soldiers working in a unit two weeks at a time.

When men were assigned from the cavalry, the officer in charge was from the artillery and vice versa. When I drew the duty and reported in, I was appalled at the slovenliness I encountered. As an Academy graduate I was deeply trained to expect clean and orderly uniforms and a military demeanor. I found neither. It was obvious the men didn't take their role as unit security members seriously. They almost treated it as a period of rest and relaxation.

With the help of a staff sergeant who was equally disappointed in the unit, I made it clear what was expected of the men while on police duty and explained the consequences if the expectations weren't met.

Soon the guards looked professional and stayed awake when making their rounds. They checked soldiers' identifications properly, saluted officers sharply. In short, they looked like a professional and capable security unit for a change.

This didn't go unnoticed. I received another commendation and was told to remain at the post another two weeks, then another month.

One day a military police colonel in U.S. Army Europe made an appointment to see me. He had an offer: there existed a vacant position normally filled by a captain. I was a first lieutenant at this time. He said if I was willing to change my military occupational specialty from Armor to MP, I could have the appointment.

I was more than a little stunned. The position was Provost Marshal of Ansbach, Germany. I would have policing authority over five Landkreises, or counties, in Ansbach, Germany in central Bavaria — a command with a complement of 45 men, the headquarters office, several cars, and four Jeeps for going on field work.

I accepted and I filled the rest of my tour of duty in that role.

During the time I was Provost Marshal I worked closely with the German civilian police force as well as the military police forces of the allied nations that were posted in my jurisdiction. Out of all this experience I started developing a keen interest in police work. In particular, I learned what policemen should and should not do or be.

As they do today, news stories abounded about police misconduct, brutality and over-reaction. It may sound simplistic but I realized then — I still do to this very day — that the answer to correcting misbehavior is loud and clear in the U.S. Navy's Leadership 101 course.

It teaches pride in one's position. It calls for daily practice of the position's requirements and responsibilities — living up to those requirements. Knowing that one has done so is absolutely essential to true leadership. It amounts to a matter of self-awareness and the exercise of conscientiousness.

I learned in Germany that police work is demanding and difficult. To be responsible for ensuring that laws and rules are followed one must in turn follow those very same laws and rules.

I told myself that upon returning to civilian life, one way or another, I would participate in law enforcement leadership.

4

Cloud over the thin blue line

The problems facing the City of Memphis and its police department in 1977 were enormous. E. Winslow (Buddy) Chapman wasn't ignorant of them. In his advisory position to the Mayor he was well informed. He had observed enough to know the police force was supremely entrenched in an "us against all of them" mentality, even as the department too often failed to carry out the basic mission of all police departments: to protect the safety of citizens and lawfully fight crime.

A short litany of challenges facing the community included:

• The city's growing financial crisis;

• Municipal labor disenchantment;

• Complaints piled on complaints about police officers mistreating and sometimes brutalizing suspects and even plain citizens, especially in the black community;

• Police manpower shortages;

• The threat of U.S. Justice Department intervention or even takeover of the city's police department.

Many of the police issues had led to lawsuits and federal investigations starting in the 1960s and up to 1977 that resulted in federal consent decrees — court ordered reform plans — covering civil rights violations. The violations involved police brutality, police spying on citizens — even Martin Luther King Jr. when visiting the city — and unlawful treatment of inmates in the city's jail.

Black community leaders were aroused and sought redress. White leaders were joining in. Washington's official eye was uncomfortably set on Memphis. Throughout the city there was a sense of something about to explode.

When Chapman left the service after four years he was returning home with a wife and newborn child. He intended to enroll in college and was accepted at several schools but chose Memphis State University (now The University of Memphis) to stay near his aging mother and the family holdings. After a year it became clear he could not meet family needs and stay in school.

He started farming. He wanted International Harvester equipment. There was no dealership in the area so he started one and called the business Windermere Equipment Company. The new concern flourished until Case Tractor acquired IH. Chapman closed the business and used the remaining equipment on the farm.

This was a period in his life when he felt the draw of politics. He joined a newly-formed Sheriff's Reserve Unit and spent a great deal of time with its members. When Dr. King was shot, he found himself assigned to street duty during the tense days that followed. When Sheriff William (Bill) Morris ran for the county mayor's seat and won in 1970, Chapman became a candidate for sheriff, still feeling the pull toward law enforcement.

He came in third place in that race. During the campaign he met a lot of people. Those relationships led to his job in city hall and finally to his appointment as police director.

*****

Chief Crumby's departure meant I finally was free to put in place police command staff made up of people I had identified as best-suited to help me move the MPD in a better direction. My plans left open the status of the three top commissioned officers. The influential International Association of Chiefs of Police had long supported civil service protection, but Crumby's tenure demonstrated the problem of ridding the department of someone you couldn't force to leave.

I decided the three ranking positions in the force would for a time be acting positions only. My choice for acting Deputy Director was a retired officer named John (Jack) Holt. He had taken early retirement because of health problems and the fact he couldn't stomach many of Crumby's actions and decisions. He didn't care about civil service protection and became my chief of operations as soon as I was named director.

Newspaper commentary thought I was on the right track by naming him to the position. In a news analysis for *The Commercial Appeal*, William Bayne wrote that "new levels of efficiency and police service are in store for Memphians … Holt is a planner and a doer…"

Bayne was right. He was all that and much more. He helped me identify individuals in the department who were ready for change and capable of carrying out my wishes. Then Bayne quoted me in that story: "For far too long in this building, the word has been power — who had it, how it was used and what you could do with it. That's out. The only word around here that carries any weight any more is responsibility. I want more command leadership around this place and I'm going to have it."

A leading citizen then and for years later — D'Army Bailey — wrote an op-ed column with the headline: "Chapman's Toughest Task Lies Ahead." Bailey said he liked hearing what I had to say but he was waiting for actions to go with the words.

It is the "dichotomy between the open and change-oriented

leadership which Chapman promises within the department, and the resistance to input from other sources outside of the department which may serve as the greatest barrier to the ultimate goal of better police-community relations," he wrote.

"Chapman is forthright and promises a new perspective in police leadership. He has weathered his first major challenge in the battle with Crumby. Now the tougher task of making positive changes within the department and bringing it closer to the citizens of Memphis lies ahead."

Bailey was absolutely correct in his assessment and he had every right to be skeptical as well as hopeful. I kept a copy of his piece — still have it — and felt obliged to live up to my own promises as well as his lofty but fair expectations.

The Tri-State Defender published an editorial that stated simply and well the problems then (and now) facing most police agencies. Under the headline, "Buddy Chapman Tackles Tough Job," it said, in part, "There exists a negative image throughout the community toward the Police Department."

How true and how precisely this zeroed in on the essential point. Public image, both factual and perceived, always hangs above police work. In 1977 it hung like a heavy black cloud.

In a second editorial, that newspaper quoted me saying, "I haven't had an easy day since I've been here. The hardest thing I've had to do, and I haven't done it yet, is to turn the department in a positive direction in the way it looks at itself. "

Early in my tenure I determined that I would keep myself always open to members of the press and TV reporters. They could almost always reach me to ask questions and report the news, good or bad. I've never regretted that decision. Police leaders who refuse to make themselves available to reporters for whatever reason take the wrong road, I believe.

Word about my perspective on working with news reporters hadn't dropped down to all the lower ranks yet.

One night I was roaming around the city in my police car doing exactly what I had said I would do: check up on what my troops were up to. I came to an I-240 bypass on the north side of town when I saw emergency lights. There had been an accident. I drove to the site of the collision and saw a Channel 5 TV News truck. When I got out of my car I saw that the reporter, whom I knew, was sitting in the back seat of a police cruiser.

"What's he doing in there?" I asked the patrolman.

"He's under arrest, sir."

"For what?"

"For taking pictures. I told him to stop and he wouldn't."

"Did he get in the way of you performing your duties?"

"No."

"Did he shine a bright light in your face?"

"Well, no."

"All right, here's what you're going to do. First, unarrest that reporter. Then I want you, your lieutenant and your union rep in my office tomorrow morning."

The next day the trio came in and I asked them to cite for me from the Tennessee Annotated Code of Statutes what the reporter had done wrong.

"Now you know, Director, there ain't no such law," the lieutenant drawled.

"That's right," I said, turning to the young officer. "I want you to understand that you can't enforce laws that don't exist."

Months later that officer came to me to say he had learned his lesson .

Would that more officers — and their command lieutenants — did. And do.

Jack Holt, now late in his career, had become my acting deputy director and he was a great "number two." He had suffered multiple heart attacks that he said "merely made me meaner," and it was clear he felt he could give only so much to a 24-hour, seven-day-per-week job. He helped me immensely and continued in a support position until he retired again in September of that year. Jack could take an abstract idea and put it to practice as well as anyone I ever worked with.

During that time Mayor Chandler announced a reorganization of the Fire and Police Departments. He established the positions of deputy directors for operations and administration for each. This step eliminated the civil service issue for each department's chief position. In consultation with Holt I named chief inspector Mickey Jones as the city's first official deputy director of the MPD. It proved a good move.

Two large issues loomed and they were interconnected: the city's fiscal and union problems.

The city was suffering financial woes. The Council announced budget cuts were to be expected and layoffs were possible. This came as negotiations were to begin with the fairly new Memphis Police Association, which was one of two groups then representing police officers. Since the negotiations were tied to a parallel set of talks with the city's sanitation workers, I wasn't directly involved.

At the same time the U.S. Commission on Civil Rights convened a panel in Memphis concerning police-community relations, which was the focus of various ongoing independent investigations of police misconduct. The three-person panel included Commission Chair Arthur S. Flemming, who came in

63

from Washington, D.C. Speakers that day and the next amounted to a who's who of Memphis then and today, including the future mayor, A C Wharton, who at that time was a public defender and director of Memphis and Shelby County Legal Services; U.S. Attorney Mike Cody; lawyer Bruce Kramer who headed the local American Civil Liberties Union; Maxine Smith, executive secretary-Memphis branch of the National Association for the Advancement of Colored People, and many more.

I began to more perfectly understand that not only was I an avowed police reformer but also a key part of the force I wanted to reform. Many of the speakers left me in no doubt of my rock and hard spot position. Wharton called my changes to date "cosmetic" and said they amounted to "reprimands and slaps on the wrists." He demanded funds from the U.S. Congress to support more local lawsuits against the police. [9]

Smith said that since I had become director of police the number of police brutality complaints had "not lessened." I testified that I was attempting to establish lines of communication in the Black community and I planned to establish a Citizen Advisory Board. I enumerated the number of misconduct cases I had referred to the U.S. Attorney's Office and to the District Attorney for prosecution of officers.[10]

I knew these and other community activists were right. But I also felt I needed more time to make lasting reforms. I knew that my future steps and actions were what mattered.

It didn't help that when it came his time to testify, Wyeth Chandler said he believed that police-community problems really

---

[9] *Memphis Press-Scimitar*, May 9, 1977
[10] Ibid

rested on "fanatic statements" made by leaders in the black community. Chandler could be a little mercurial at times. He didn't appreciate the way the Civil Rights Commission gave a sounding board to leading activists. It was true that some of them made outrageous statements now and then. But many of the police actions were themselves outrageous.

Not one person in those hearings believed there wasn't a problem with police misconduct. The reality of systemic police brutality became apparent once more in a series of incidents that summer, inflaming the Black community and all those focused on how police officers conducted themselves.

First, the city had two successive "fleeing felon" shootings.

Then an off-duty officer was charged with first-degree murder in a shooting that followed an argument and left a 21-year-old man dead. In another case, a woman brandishing a shotgun was shot and killed by a patrolman arriving on the scene of a domestic argument. Altogether that summer, four Black citizens were killed by Memphis police officers in various incidents. Meanwhile, two officers were fired after an excessive use of force incident inside the jail earlier in March. The jail then was under the control of the MPD.

Conditions in the community worsened in August when the officers who had been fired for beating an inmate, were reinstated by the Civil Service Commission, infuriating the city. Commissioners still were intervening in too many disciplinary cases.

"Who Runs The Police" asked a headline in *The Commercial Appeal*. The editorial pointed out that the police director needed the latitude to punish misconduct without being second-guessed by a union or by Civil Service commissioners. The piece also pointed

65

out that lethal force sometimes is necessary in certain police encounters. The idea that an officer should "shoot to wound" — a rule some activists wanted installed — is absurd, the piece added. Another of my favorite editorial cartoons appeared. It depicted me with a sizable lump on my skull, leaning on a police precinct desk and saying, "I've been mugged."[11]

On August 10, 1977, U.S. Justice Department officials were in Memphis for a meeting with black leaders. Assistant U.S. Attorney Gen. Drew Days told them the federal government planned to clamp down on unjustified police shootings in the city. The meeting had been requested and organized by U.S. Attorney Cody. He worried that tensions in the community were dangerously high. Cody said he believed the Justice Department was not intent on taking over the local police department but wanted to lend support and assure the community that their concerns were being heard.

The city later would learn just how close the federal government came to taking charge here.

One thing I thought was clear: things were going to get out of control if lasting changes didn't occur soon. One step I announced at that meeting was a directive to police that in any potential conflict with an armed individual, the department's tactical squad should be called in first if possible.

I met the next day with Maxine Smith. I quickly learned that she (and this was true for her husband Vasco) was someone I could work with. She could be fiery and had a no-nonsense attitude when she felt it was needed. She also was a fair-minded person with a sense of humor and a willingness to give someone like me a chance to make change.

---

[11] *The Commercial Appeal*, August 9, 1977

Reforms, though hard to bring about, were sorely needed. I knew this now more than ever, as did a growing number of community leaders and the public.

It was an obvious fact that the force had some officers who clearly exhibited the attitudes of a certain mold referred to internally as the "real police." The term referred to policemen willing and capable of meting out their own justice if they felt disrespected. These were white officers who harbored deep racial prejudice and had personal tendencies toward violence and brutality.

Police training at that time was fairly good and would get much better over the years. But too often a recruit would graduate to a police cruiser where he was told by an older officer, "Hey, forget all that training stuff. Let me tell you the truth about police work."

It also was true, however, that there were exemplary officers in the force. It would help, I believed and said often, if leaders in the Black community showed support of efforts to correct problems. Many did.

I had promised to create an advisory group and I carried through on that promise even though the Mayor at first opposed the concept. Henry Evans supported me and Chandler relented. I wanted to bring to the new Police Advisory Council voices and points of view from across the spectrum of community leaders and activists. I made every effort to gain diversity in the group. A member of Chandler's staff told me later that I probably was the only person in the State of Tennessee who could have gotten members of the White Citizen's Council and representatives of the African-American Ajanaku Family to sit down at a table and talk to each other. I didn't mention to Chandler that I was giving the advisory council the ability to address any situation or set of circumstances as long as an ongoing investigation or case wouldn't be jeopardized. Their job only was to make recommendations; I would decide whether and how to act.

As it turned out, the formation of this group was extremely helpful. It helped us immensely with the Justice Department by demonstrating we were trying to live up to the various consent decrees. There were times when some members of the Advisory Council wanted to play heavier roles — giving me directives instead of recommendations. But those people would ultimately quit the body when they learned they weren't in charge. The Council met with me often. I was accused at times of preaching to members a little too much about policing, but I felt they had to have a full picture in order to give me recommendations worth considering.

That year seemed to be crammed day to day with new issues and problems to solve. But Tuesday, August 16, 1977 brought a unique set of circumstances.

I was in a meeting in City Hall with Mayor Chandler and the Director of Fire Services Robert Walker when Walker's beeper sounded. It was a signal of a serious emergency. He left to make a call and came back in.

"Mayor," he said quietly. "They just transported Elvis to the hospital, only this time he didn't make it."

It wasn't widely known then but Elvis Presley was a heavy user, even abuser of prescription medications — opiates, barbiturates and sedatives. He had been admitted so often to Baptist Memorial Hospital that they had a room set aside for him. The report said he died of a heart attack brought on by an overdose of medicines. The toxicology report later showed his system contained a real witche's brew of drugs, including high dosages of Dilaudid, Percodan, Demerol, Quaaludes and Codeine.

I knew what the news of this icon's death meant for the city.

I hastily called for my top staff to be assembled and we met at police headquarters. We put together an operational plan for crowd control and various other services. I then drove to Graceland. By that time the crowd of people was so large that the highway in front of the mansion was already blocked. Throughout the afternoon more people came.

I remember wondering at how quiet they were for such a large number of people. As more people came walking up from wherever they had parked their cars it was obvious we had a problem in the making. While we set up detours on either side of the crowd, people close to the stone wall in front of Graceland were starting to get crushed, pushed not on purpose by the mass of people behind them.

We had to resort to a maneuver called "combing the crowd." That involves lining up horses and motorcycles to literally push through to create space so that people can move and breathe. We brought in dozens of motorcycle policemen. The procedure is usually used in riots or for mob control and can result in people getting angry and injured.

Not this time. People were completely cooperative. They realized they needed to move back and quickly did, even as more people filled the area all the way up and down the highway in front of the grounds, and well across the road.

Seeing a long night was before us, I set up my own command post in a hallway to the rear of the house in order to be out of the way. George Klein was receiving close associates and family members at the front of the house. The body was brought in. I settled by the stairway that led to the famous Jungle Room, using a phone and my police radio to hear progress reports.

About 8 p.m. Elvis's cook came out of the nearby kitchen and asked if she could fix me anything to eat. Although I hadn't eaten since early in the day I told her I didn't want to put her to any trouble. She said she couldn't leave and she was bored. She went back to the kitchen and soon brought me a steak. It seemed I had no choice, so I sat near the entrance to the Jungle Room and ate a delicious steak supper.

It started raining as the night went on but no one in the crowd left. We had arranged for two media tents to be built. By now journalists were arriving from all over.

About midnight I took a walk around the grounds and to check the situation at the main gate. If anything, the crowd was even bigger. Motorcycle officers were still doing their work. People mainly were just standing in the rain, looking toward the home of the beloved Elvis Presley. Near the front gate I saw a young woman who looked familiar. After a few minutes I decided it was Caroline Kennedy. I approached her and she confirmed who she was and said she was there reporting for *Rolling Stone* magazine but that no one would accept her credentials.

I told the officers at the gate to let her in and motioned to her to go to one of the media tents. Instead she went directly to the front door, explained who she was and made her way inside.

I was told later — by George Klein, who let her in — that she didn't mention she was there in a reporting capacity and so the Graceland entourage thought she was representing the Kennedy family. She spent the next hours mingling with the Presley family, including Priscilla and Lisa Marie, father Vernon, aunts and others, and viewing Elvis's swollen face in a copper casket. She certainly got her story.

In her article she said I looked like the "advance man" from the movie *Nashville*. She misstated that I let her into the house, though.[12] My friend George Klein always gave me a hard time over that incident.

The next days seemed larger than life, as the saying goes. There were private family gatherings and ceremonies, and the very public funeral procession to Forest Hill Cemetery. It took about 100 vans just to carry all the flowers sent from around the world. Every motorcade needed police escorts.

That wasn't the end of the saga. The remains of Elvis's mother were moved to be near Elvis but that was done without the required permits under Tennessee law. Then on the night of August 28 four men attempted to steal Elvis's body to hold it for ransom. At one point a national publication attempted to pay money to obtain a copy of the autopsy report. Although it isn't easy to do, the family was able to obtain a permit to locate the gravesites on the grounds of Elvis's estate. The remains of Elvis Presley, along with those of his mother, were moved to Graceland and eventually became part of the mansion tour and a focal point for annual tributes every August during "death week."

Soon after I was named director, I received an invitation to the annual meeting of the International Association of Chiefs of Police. The group had a subset known as the Major Cities Chiefs, made up of police leaders in cities of a population of 500,000 or more. I was particularly interested in participating in that group.

But Bill Crumby in a sense got there before me.

Ed Davis, the legendary police chief of Los Angeles, headed the Major Cities panel that year. In the very first meeting he told

---

[12] *Rolling Stone*, September 22, 1977

me I shouldn't be there because my title was director and not chief. He said this even though the group included a sheriff from Jacksonville-Duvall County Metro Department, the sheriff of Los Angeles County, the superintendent of police from Philadelphia and the commissioner of police from New Orleans.

Davis went on to say that he had talked to Chief Bill Crumby and that it was he who should be representing Memphis. Davis went out of his way to be unpleasant to me throughout the meetings. On the afternoon of the second day, I'd had enough.

I stood up in the meeting and said it was obvious he didn't appreciate my presence at the meeting. "I'm leaving," I said. "But if this group wants representation from Memphis, it will be me or nobody."

At this point, Sheriff Peter Pitchess of Los Angeles County — a legend in his own right — stood and told me to wait. Turning to Davis, he said, "Ed, you dumb son of a bitch. The young man is trying to tell you something: you don't get to decide who will be a member of this organization. As far as I am concerned, Director Chapman, you are more than welcome."

There were murmurs of assent around the room.

I tell this particular story because Sheriff Pete Pitchess and I became close friends and we visited on many occasions. He had been a retired FBI agent on the West Coast before becoming sheriff and knew a lot of people, including celebrities.

In particular, he knew an actor named Ronald Reagan quiet well. When Pete was appointed by President Reagan to the White House Advisory Council on Law Enforcement, he got me invited onto the Council as well.

That would prove beneficial to Memphis.

5

Running the gauntlet

Several months into his job as Memphis police director, Buddy Chapman could see just how many battlefronts he was engaged in fighting. The Crumby fight was behind him. Ahead were countless obstacles and challenges to police reform.

He had a police force too small for the size of the city. Officers were underpaid compared to those of most other police forces its size and no chance for pay increases could be seen in the foreseeable future because of tight finances in city government. Many officers were disgruntled about the lack of promotion and looked toward union membership for help. Chapman also still had within the ranks officers who had been involved in harassing people or worse. The number of police beatings under investigation was mounting. He was slowly bringing about meaningful reforms to a force that was entrenched in past policies, procedures and practices. But change takes time and study.

Each new idea or change also had to have buy-in from ranking commanders, some of whom were slowly warming to the concept of reform.

Meanwhile, Chapman was fully engaged in meetings on community complaints and attending well-organized civil rights investigations and hearings. Every evening and early in the mornings he closely read the newspapers for opinions, insights and reporting. He didn't want to miss anything.

He also believed that good ideas could come from anywhere.

In February of 1978 the first fruits of his association with the newly organized U.S. Law Enforcement Assistance Administration were ripening. Memphis was one of 31 cities in the country chosen to implement what became the Integrated Criminal Apprehension Program, or ICAP. Federal funding made it possible for Chapman to establish the Crime Analysis Center.

Today it's called the Real Time Crime Center.

*****

That first LEAA grant would give us a big chance to modernize our investigative procedures. We purchased computer equipment in order to collect data on all Class One (the most serious) felonies committed in Memphis. We used the statistics to model areas of criminal activity so that the allocation of resources could follow the data. For the first time it was possible to detect patterns and methods of operation by burglars and other thieves.

The data further enabled us to train officers in the field in better methods for conducting investigations, freeing the detective division to handle major mystery crimes. Writing in the *Memphis Press-Scimitar*, reporter Menno Duerkson said ICAP could result "in a revolutionary change in police department operations."

He wasn't exaggerating. But reform can be one step forward, two steps the other direction.

The operating budget submitted by Mayor Chandler to the city council in May of 1978 was one of the most austere budgets the city had seen in many years. To reach balance it called for no increase in taxation and foresaw no increase in funds from other sources such as payments in lieu of taxation.

A month before, a class of 47 new police officers was sworn in. They were the first to be added in two years but no additional classes were under consideration and the MPD was 50 officers below 1975 numbers.

There were a lot of downcast faces during the budget hearings that year. I added to the somber atmosphere no doubt when I met with the City Council. The police department is on the "ragged edge" of a manpower shortage that is "sapping its ability to protect," I said. "I can and I will operate the department on this budget but I would be remiss in my responsibility to the citizens of Memphis if I did not point out what this means."

To blunt the impact of a tight budget I looked for ways to do business better. I started an exploratory look into the possibility of ranking and prioritizing calls. I ordered the department to find ways to reduce response time. Quietly, I also began considering moving to patrolling with one officer in squad cars instead of a pair.

It wasn't yet time to do that, but I knew it probably was inevitable and of course that's normal today.

Firefighters and police personnel were making unhappy noises. They felt misunderstood and unappreciated. They were unhappy about salaries, pensions and promotions and the lack of meaningful compensation for injuries on the job. Union trouble was in the wind.

The Tennessee advisory committee to the U.S. Commission on Civil Rights continued conducting hearings on police-community relations. The Chairman was the Rev. Samuel (Billy) Kyles who, after more testimony from citizens, said what was lacking in the police force was professionalism.

Mayor Chandler refused to meet with the group, calling them "a bunch of weirdoes" and saying its work amounted to a witchhunt. I agreed to meet with the committee twice and tried to point out that most of what the committee was hearing about was from the past and was being addressed.

The committee and I were definitely moving at cross-purposes. Its report to the full commission focused on past leadership of the Memphis Police. Its title really said it all: "Civic Crisis-Civic Challenge: Police-Community Relations in Memphis." In turn, Bobby Doctor, the Southern Regional Director for the U.S. Commission, proclaimed that police misconduct goes virtually unpunished in Memphis and will threaten future federal funding.

The *Press-Scimitar* called the report "phony rhetoric." Its editorial said the reported civil rights charges were "tied to a false assumption — that Memphians tolerate police abuses. We are quite sure that public opinion leans heavily against police misbehavior of any kind."

Meanwhile I needed to address problems at the City Jail. (The jail later would be transferred to Shelby County government as part of the Criminal Justice Center.) Because I had built a reputation of being open and accessible, people were beginning to bring problems to my attention — problems that heretofore were swept under the proverbial police rug.

The MPD sat under one federal consent decree stemming from a lawsuit that claimed inmates were being subjected to cruel, unusual and unlawful conditions. I had gotten several specific reports that indicated the proper handling of prisoners wasn't being followed and that the reports of abuse were likely true. Since it now was a matter before the U.S. District Court, I met with the city attorney and told him I intended to place an undercover agent into the jail disguised as a prisoner.

He concurred with my plan and I had the individual booked into the jail under fictitious charges and using an alias. As a result of the undercover man's stay in jail, six employees faced charges and a criminal investigation was started into the illegal solicitation of bonds through bail bond companies in league with jailers. To keep the pressure on, I publicly announced my intention to place more agents in the jail.

Although I believed I had reached an understanding with the U.S. Civil Rights Commission's Southern Division about the steps we were taking, in January of 1979 Washington officials showed up in Memphis with the intent to search the Memphis Police Department's Internal Affairs Bureau files. This resulted from the report from the Division's Tennessee Advisory Committee that claimed police misconduct goes virtually unpunished especially when brutality charges are involved.

A legal brouhaha quickly developed. The Memphis Police Association took the position that officer statements taken in the course of internal investigations didn't carry a Miranda rights provision. The Mayor took issue with allowing free access to the files. Attorneys for the Civil Rights Division insisted they had the authority to halt the payment of some $11 million a year in federal grants coming to Memphis unless the city cooperated.

I later reviewed what they wanted to see and it mainly was statistics on the number of complaints Internal Affairs had received, how many were investigated and the results of those investigations since 1975. Clearly it related to the earlier consent decree concerning police brutality and they should have had the right to inspect the data. They got them of course.

Not two weeks later the question of police brutality went from the abstract to the very real.

It was a cold Thursday morning in February. A man's body was found in a pile of snow in Overton Park, the city's central parkland. William (Jack) Frost was a well-known fixture in the Midtown area of Memphis. He worked odd jobs and ran errands. He also had a drinking problem and routinely got himself arrested.

Just before midnight the police got a call about an intoxicated man lying in the foyer of an apartment building near the park. Two officers about to get off duty were dispatched. Two witnesses saw what happened next.

They said the patrolmen picked the man up and hustled him into the squad car and then left the scene. Later there was no record that they had made an arrest. Further investigation produced witnesses who heard sounds of someone being beaten. The man pleaded, "Don't hit me again," they said. The medical examiner ruled that he had died from exposure to the elements but that he bore signs of having been severely beaten beforehand.

Bloodstains were discovered in the cruiser. More blood was on one officer's nightstick. As both men had records of having used excessive force in the past, they were immediately suspended and subsequently fired and indicted for second-degree murder. This was one of the most egregious cases brought to my attention at this point, and yet a jury later only found the men guilty of dereliction of duty for not processing him properly. The two men sought reinstatement on the force.

It wouldn't be the only time indicted officers had been set free by juries during my tenure.

Two other officers had been charged with using excessive force in the arrest of a 20-year-old in January of 1977. In 1978 a federal court jury ruled in their favor after only 35 minutes deliberation. Another man arrested for hitchhiking in 1977 got two broken arms and a broken finger while in custody in the jail. He was granted $1,000 for his injuries but the officer was returned to duty. In a few other cases, though, officers were convicted of charges.

At least I was given the opportunity to demonstrate to both the police force and to the community how I would take corrective action and order punishment in an instance of police brutality.

In November of 1978 I was scheduled to meet with Bobby Doctor and Rev. Kyles and a stormy time was predicted. Instead, committee officials generally praised my efforts to improve relations between the police department and the community. Doctor announced that for the city to move to a better place "everyone will have to recognize that it is everyone's problem — not just Buddy Chapman's."

That meeting was held in the wake of one of the darkest times in the city's history — bitter and prolonged strikes by firefighters and police officers, a dangerous period coming 10 years after the grim days of 1968. And yet — out of literal ashes arose more modern and more professional Memphis Fire and Police Departments.

In the end, it would mean a slightly less bumpy road to reform for me.

6

Serve and protect
— except on strike

A Delta jet took off from the Memphis airport early July 1, 1978, and headed north to Chicago. Looking out the windows, passengers could see black smoke wafting up from dozens of sites in the city. They were like smoke signals. In fact that's exactly what they were: fires started by men who usually can be counted on to put fires out. The smoke was meant to send a message.

The International Association of Fire Fighters Local 1784 voted late the previous night to strike over wages, work conditions and other frustrations dating back several years. For the next four days, arson fires would spring up downtown and in the suburbs. Supervisory personnel tried to rush to various fires, ultimately having to put abandoned buildings down the list of priority. Many burned to the ground.

National Guardsmen were brought into the city for the second time in a decade. Strict curfews hurt businesses. A court order had the firefighters back on the job in four days, but after weeks of mediation, wildcat walkouts and picketing, the police went on strike and fire personnel joined them.

In many ways it was a lost summer.

But the smell of burned buildings wasn't the only thing in the air. Change was coming.

*****

The city's firefighters voted unanimously to reject the city's final contract offer the night of Friday, June 30, 1978. The strike was set to begin the next morning, with pickets at every firehouse. "If they go out, we will handle it," Mayor Chandler said. He made plans to provide emergency services if the strike went on and firehouses were left empty.

Negotiations still were under way with the Memphis Police Association and the American Federation of State, County and Municipal Employees. AFSCME said its members wouldn't work without a contract. Police representatives said they wouldn't walk out if a deadline passed without agreement.

Firefighters, like other employees, insisted on better pay raises than offered by the city. They also had certain "shift differential" demands and raised other issues such as long hours and lack of compensation for injuries.

The mood wasn't pretty and soon would get much worse.

When fire personnel didn't report to work the next day, and fire alarms started to come in, a state of civil emergency was declared in Memphis, with a 10 p.m. to 6 a.m. curfew. The National Guard was alerted. Supervising fire personnel and a few non-strikers assumed fire-fighting duties, assisted by 860 members of the Army and Air National Guard working 12-hour shifts.

The first night, scores of fires started before the curfew took effect. The next night more fires erupted. Most of the fires had been set intentionally. Soon scores of buildings, most abandoned, were ablaze around the city. Over the next few days the fires continued. One fire set the old wooden Nutrena Mill building near downtown ablaze. Smoke billowed over the city and the Mississippi River as it became one of the biggest fires in Memphis since the Russwood Park baseball stadium burned down, threatening Baptist Hospital in 1960. Even worse was the loss of the historic Vance Public Library building, a prize in the black community.

Accelerants were used to start many of the fires. Fingers pointed to striking firefighters. At one point a fire started in front of City Hall. It was put out but not before the marble façade blackened in one spot. It was clear that the fires were arson and I believed many had been selected to burn before the strike began. In a 24-hour period from July 1 to July 2 there were 225 calls to fires. Twelve of them were classified as major fires.

The New York Times took note of the strike in a July 2 edition. The story quoted Chandler as saying that "the nuts ran wild in our community last night and early today."

As the nation watched the next five days of turmoil in the city, commentary largely opposed the strike and union tactics. *The Dallas Morning News* summed up well what other news organizations were saying in editorials: "The unionizing of public employees has always been dangerous in principal, for reasons that should be clear now. When public employees strike, they strike not against their management but against the public itself. It is well to remember the statement of Calvin Coolidge during a police strike in Boston. 'There is no right to strike against the public safety by anybody, anywhere, anytime.' That is as true in 1978 as it was in 1919."

In Memphis the firefighters union issued a statement that "spontaneous combustion" in the summer heat no doubt was the cause of many fires. No one believed that. In fact, a few firefighters were arrested and charged with arson.

Although the AFSCME ratified a contract with the city, most members refused to go to work for several days in consideration of the striking firefighters. Garbage began to pile up in the city. The police agreed to return to their negotiating table although no date was set. Meanwhile merchants and businesses throughout the city were forecasting dire financial circumstances if the strike and emergency conditions continued.

In keeping with Chandler's curfew order, I issued rules of enforcement. They included:

• All persons found in the streets during curfew hours were subject to questioning, search and arrest;

• All retail establishments or businesses catering directly to the public were required to close during curfew hours with certain exceptions: hospitals, pharmacies and other emergency service facilities, public transportation services, security firms and news businesses.

Employees of those groups could go about their normal duties but had to carry satisfactory identification papers subject to review by police or National Guard troops.

Another complicated set of rules governed other businesses, including manufacturing and production facilities. The sale of gasoline or other flammable liquids was prohibited except for fueling motor vehicles. During curfew hours the sale or use of alcohol or weapons were severely restricted.

By Monday the wave of structure fires had turned the city "into a scene like a World War II newsreel," the *Press-Scimitar* reported.[13]

The fire union proclaimed it did not condone arson. The fires should be blamed on "arsonists who are not firemen," it said in a statement. Sam Posey, the union's vice president, said officials "stressed to the membership to 'act like professionals.'" When

---

[13] *Memphis Press-Scimitar*, July 3, 1978

news reporters reminded Posey that firefighters had been arrested and charged with arson, he replied, "We cannot control 1,400 people."

That certainly was true.

A Chancery Court order told fire strikers to return to work. The executive board of the union recommended compliance. Members shouted them down and threw insults at Wyeth Chandler and myself. The members left that meeting in a subdued mood but vowed they wouldn't throw out their signs. Negotiations were set to resume that Wednesday, July 5, to discuss inviting a federal mediator to help.

That day, the city announced that initial estimates showed about $6 million in fire damages had been tallied so far.

The police union was holding daily meetings and hearing from its members. Police officers reporting to work on July 4 had to go to other locations for roll call because picket lines were established by firefighters at each precinct. The fire union learned the pickets violated the court's injunction and so they were scaled back to "information only" pickets. That day the court ordered an end to the strike, and most firefighters obeyed grumpily. In their hearts they were still on strike and ready for more action.

By now Gen. Carl Wallace, commanding the Tennessee National Guard, said he had 1,108 troops on duty with few conflicts. Strikers had prevented fire trucks from responding to fires a few times, Wallace said, but the curfew was effective. Twenty-one people were arrested for violating the curfew hours the first night but only 10 the second.

The troops were gradually pulled from the city's streets, but the atmosphere throughout the city remained tense. Firemen were back on the job but disgruntled as union leaders, city officials and mediators continued talking. And union leaders for the police and firefighters shared information regularly.

A closed-door meeting with mediator Lonnie Stokes was set Thursday, July 6, at 10 a.m. The afternoon newspaper quickly filed a lawsuit contending the state's Sunshine Law meant the meeting should be open to the press. In its suit the *Press-Scimitar's* lawyer said, "The public will sustain irreparable damages as a result if the defendants refuse to comply with the Sunshine Law." To the surprise of many, Special Chancellor John C. Robertson agreed. He issued a temporary restraining order barring closed-door bargaining sessions and ordered the city to allow qualified members of the news media to attend.[14]

During a meeting I had at the same time with police union team member David Baker I learned that the police wanted their own federal mediator. It was clear to me that no real progress was under way on any front.

Baker explained the problem with the city's offer this way: Proposed increases compared unfavorably to raises for other public employees. "County employees," he said, "received a 7 percent raise. Deputy sheriffs received 8 percent, Light Gas and Water got 7.5 percent." He added that many factories in the city were averaging 7.3 percent raises. He noted that the cost of living had risen that year by 6.5 percent, a rise that the city's offer of 6 percent wouldn't offset.

"The public needs to know that bus drivers make more than policemen do. I'm not knocking bus drivers but on the same scale they make $7.09 an hour and policemen make $6.62."

The Sunshine Law ruling was proving to be a big hurdle for everyone. The city called for a special hearing and Chancellor

---

[14] *Memphis Press-Scimitar,* July 6, 1978

Robertson agreed to consider again whether firefighters' bargaining sessions would be open to public scrutiny or if the press could be kept out. Brady Bartusch, representing City Hall, told Robertson that although both the city and union were interested in getting the matter settled, until the open or closed question was solved there would be no more formal talks. Attorneys for both sides argued that the Sunshine Law applied to legislative bodies, not administrative or negotiating team meetings. Further, Bartusch said, the newspaper had not shown what irreparable harm would be done if reporters were excluded.

After hearing the arguments, the Chancellor cancelled his order. There was no reduction in the newspapers' expenditure of paper and ink in covering the news the rest of that summer.

The next day the city and Memphis Police Association agreed to federal mediators. Baker (by now union president) and I made the announcement in a press conference. During it Baker said he wanted to quell rumors of a job action by police. I agreed that the new negotiating phase might clear the air.

My next meeting was with General William Kinton of the National Guard. He had been chosen to work with me on a contingency plan in case a police strike came about. The plan called for deploying Tennessee Highway Patrol officers and Shelby County deputy sheriff's around the community.

With that help, alongside the National Guardsmen, I realized we could keep peace and secure public safety. The fire strike situation was different. Who other than firefighters could operate equipment and fight blazes? About 225 supervisors worked long hours during the strike. Fortunately, the arsons had stopped.

The business of policing, of course, continued during this time. A record seizure of cocaine on August 7 had a street value of

$1.8 million. A major drug ring in the city was broken up by arrests. There even was a bit of humor from time to time.

A member of the MPD took a vacation with his family to Disney World. He came back with Mickey Mouse hats for the "muckety-mucks" of the command staff, including myself. *The Commercial Appeal* reported we all had been enrolled in the Mickey Mouse Club. A cartoon showed me, of course, wearing the ears.[15]

Talks with the unions were going nowhere as days seemed to slowly creep past.

At this stage I was certain the police would strike. I had been successful reaching the department's command structure. Many were buying in to the concept of reform and understood the process could be achingly slow. The rest of the officers were another matter. Quite a few younger officers had joined during Chief Lux's command. They liked his plans to revamp the department with stricter hiring requirements and revised promotion opportunities. The new hires felt they had been misled when Crumby took charge and brought back the old guard.

The pandemonium surrounding Gen. Hubbard's time left the lower ranks feeling under-appreciated and misunderstood. I had written about these very problems when I pursued a Master's Degree in Justice Administration. I concluded in that essay that danger is afoot when police officers feel isolated, and when they decide that "civilians" — the public, that is — don't understand what they do and how hard their jobs are. The pre-strike emotions fit what I wrote in the dissertation years before.

I believed I was doing everything I could to mitigate the problem. I had been able to whittle down the overload of police

---

[15] *The Commercial Appeal* (Backdrop article), August 6, 1978

brass through attrition, but I was barred from making promotions throughout the force by the many lawsuits that challenged the qualifications for promotion method adopted by the city. To the men in the ranks (there were few women yet in the department), the lack of promotions was a big blow to morale.

I was quoted by the *Press-Scimitar* as saying that if I had been police director when the union organizing began, I didn't believe it would have been formed.[16] Was I right? I don't know, but I would have tried to help the rank and file if I had had the chance. But in August 1978 I was one of the main faces representing the opposition.

The Mayor, who at this time certainly was in a law and order mood, decided he would become directly involved in the negotiations. He rejected the latest proposal from the police union and said he would cancel recognition of the union if a strike were called.

The two sides really weren't so far apart on the pay scale. The union wanted 7 percent and the city was offering 6.653 percent raises. But the city now was demanding a two-year contract at that rate. The union took a vote and declared the offer "totally unacceptable."

A strike was called and at 11 p.m. on August 10 picket lines were formed around City Hall, the imposing police headquarters building and the four precincts. Firefighters soon joined the strike in support.

Once more a civil emergency was declared and a curfew ordered — this time starting at 8 p.m. and ending at 6 a.m. Our plan was put into effect and soon a long line of military vehicles was on the way to Memphis from Camp Shelby in Mississippi,

---

[16] *Memphis Press-Scimitar*, August 1, 1978

where military equipment was stored. An initial contingent of 600 National Guards returned under Gov. Ray Blanton's orders.

Union leaders promised good behavior but soon there were reports of incidents around the city. Many of the picketers were in civilian clothes but were carrying sidearms. Police cruisers were damaged and some disabled and placed across precinct driveways. At the North Precinct station a reporter said he was threatened, "You are making us nervous and if you don't leave we will make you worse than nervous."

The families of non-striking officers were visited or called on the phone and threatened. There were some instances of physical contact, including pushing, shoving and verbal taunts.

An order from Chancery Court for the strike to end was ignored. Picket signs displayed how patrolmen felt. One said, "Crime doesn't pay. Neither does police work." Another: "You wouldn't risk your life for a million bucks. A police officer does it for a lot less."

To protect supervisory police officers driving in squad cars, I assigned two Guardsmen in each car.

Just before midnight on August 12 an ultimatum was delivered to the police: "Obey the court and return to work, or be removed from the city's payroll." Strikers were given 24 hours to comply. The Mayor clarified what that meant. He said neither he nor City Council would be able to grant amnesty in the future if the order wasn't followed.

Hundreds of police officers headed downtown where union president Baker was prepared to read the order and explain what it meant. He stood on the steps in front of police headquarters. As he spoke he was shouted at and booed by the angry men in no mood to give in. As he tried to continue he suddenly was shoved away by

Chris Cothran, who had been an unsuccessful candidate for Baker's position. Baker shoved back but the police yelled they wanted to hear Cothran, so Baker threw his hands up in apparent disgust and walked away.

Cothran said he was taking over from Baker. "There's no doubt in anybody's mind who's running this union," he shouted to cheers. "The men are tired of finding out what their future holds from the newspapers and television. I tell you right now the Memphis Police Association is still on strike.

"If we are going to be arrested we're going to be arrested by Memphis Police officers. We are not going to be arrested by reserves. We're not going to be arrested by deputy sheriffs, and if the National Guard wants another war —"

A roar from the crowd interrupted his words. Everyone knew what he meant.

I watched everything from a perch in City Hall.

As the crowd milled about and grew, first-floor windows inside police headquarters were being boarded from the inside. Riflemen were stationed at windows on the top floor. Across what was then known as Mid-America Mall, security guards armed with shotguns stood at every entrance.

The city was as close to anarchy as it ever was, except perhaps during the worst times of the yellow fever epidemics.

Cothran was urging the crowd to be peaceful but that proved difficult. Around the city nails were thrown on the streets outside precincts. The stations mainly housed high-ranking officers and the few patrolmen who refused to strike. Sometime after midnight I met briefly with Cothran, who soon would give up the control he wrested from Baker. He asked if tear gas would be used against his men. I told him we only would do that if the situation got out of control. He again moved among the policemen and urged calm.

The next two days alternated from calm to near riots. National Guard troops returned, fully equipped with riot gear and carrying plenty of ammunition. They and non-union police arrested about 50 strikers. Rocks were thrown through downtown windows and at least one shot was fired toward City Hall. A lot of the strikers were consuming alcohol.

Anger swept through the ranks of picketing police when a few of their comrades attempted to show up for work at the precincts. City officials talked constantly with firefighters' union representatives in the hopes of preventing a walkout. But after an early morning meeting on August 15, the men declared a wildcat strike.[17]

Firefighters joined the police picket lines but others were opposed to striking. Some firemen were arrested for curfew violations.

Mayor Chandler called a press conference in the afternoon. He said that although "about 100 firemen" had reported to work they had been told to go home because of continuing threats against them and their families. Chandler said, "As anyone can see, it's now an attempt by the fire and police unions, singularly and in concert, to simply close down all operations, governmental and otherwise, in our city."

By now about 1,300 Guardsmen were in the city. Tennessee's adjutant general said they would stay as long as needed, with fresh troops coming in from Cookeville, Chattanooga and Dresden.

Despite all the chaos, Graceland prepared for an influx of Elvis fans for the first anniversary of his death. Contract security was brought in for crowd control and the general keeping of the

---

[17] A wildcat strike is a walkout without official union sanction.

peace in the Whitehaven neighborhood.

Then, as if the city didn't already have enough to contend with, came the infamous city blackout. It was about 12:32 a.m. August 16 when electricity failed throughout the city and lights went out everywhere. Most people suspected union sabotage of the power grid as for two hours utility workers tried to find the source of the trouble. The problem turned out to be much more benign and a bit ridiculous.

A private security guard at a switching station had thrown a main switch in order to cut off lights above him so he could get a bit of sleep. That switch caused a domino effect of overloads and shut down the entire distribution system. That supplied another bit of jailhouse humor in the midst of a very tense time.

As talks stalled and the City said it would follow through on threats to hold strikers in contempt, the president of the AFL-CIO Labor Council warned that his 60,000 workers would "shut the city down" if the city withdrew recognition of the unions. Gov. Blanton announced he was willing to set up a three-member committee to look at binding arbitration as a way to end the strike. He added that so far the City of Memphis owed state taxpayers nearly $1 million for the use of the Tennessee National Guard.

The Mayor refused the offer. He made another offer to the unions. They rejected it. But a breakthrough was imminent.

City officials, unable to do their customary work, waited as intense negotiation began Thursday morning, August 17. The meeting included leaders of the two unions, Labor Council officials and two federal mediators. They met at the AFL-CIO's Labor Education Center. The purpose was to develop a joint proposal that would resolve contract differences and make a presentation to the city.

Discussions went through the day and well into the night, and then resumed the following day. Mayor Chandler, who wasn't expecting a truce, spent the time meeting with business owners, the restaurant association and other business and labor leaders. He agreed to meet with about 100 members of the Memphis Ministers Association who wanted the sides to find a way out. About mid-day Friday he started a seven-hour session with labor leaders and a settlement was reached that evening. After a week-long strike, policemen began to return to duty with the midnight shift.

The end left Chandler and me in somewhat different places. We agreed that none of the strikers would be punished only for being on strike. But he went even further. Despite all of his public rhetoric, he now felt it was time to close the book on bygone troubles.

I on the other hand had been somewhat closer to all the strike events, got the daily incident reports, heard first-hand about threats made. I had promised that appropriate action, including dismissal, would occur for any police officer who committed clearly illegal acts. The word "amnesty" had widely been discussed but never showed up in any final documents.

I was summoned to the Mayor's office. He reiterated that he wanted no officers disciplined for "simply being on strike." I argued and insisted that some actions were so egregious that they had to be addressed. I gave examples.

I could overlook what could be considered minor infractions, such as a returning patrolmen who misunderstood talk he heard on his police radio and jumped out of the squad car and stabbed all four of the tires in the heat of the moment. What I thought more criminal were threats against non-striking officers and their families. Some of these were very serious and led to resignations.

Our meeting became heated. By the end we agreed that I would name a five-person trial board made up of commanding officers to review the facts of each case brought to our attention. The review recommended charges against 23 individuals but generated a firestorm of protests from the union. Other local unions joined in the protests. The police union even threatened renewed job action of some kind.

I attempted to explain my position in interviews with the press. At one point I said, "It's a clear-cut issue. Either the city and citizens control the police department or labor controls the police department. I am determined it is going to be the citizens that control it." The trial board was set to convene but Chandler ordered a postponement. He held a meeting with union officials, his staff and some prominent citizens. Afterward, he said that eight of the charges should go forward and the rest should be dismissed.

His decision allayed further talk of a strike or walkout.

The cases were concluded on September 27. The results: five officers were fired, one was suspended for nine days and two were cleared of wrongdoing. The union appealed on behalf of the individuals and the Mayor conducted that meeting. In October, he overturned the terminations and suspended each for six months without pay plus another six months of probation.

In an editorial *The Commercial Appeal* asked if there existed "A Double Standard?" The piece opened with this succinct comment: "The Memphis policemen who screamed 'foul' when Police Director E W. Chapman fired five of their fellow officers for breaking department rules during the recent strike put themselves in an awkward position, to say the least, compared with routine police demands for swift and certain punishment of citizens who break the law."

The newspaper reported that there was talk I might resign since I didn't seem to have the Mayor's full support. I was often asked about that. I chose to be philosophical. I knew all along that his was the final word on any action and I anticipated the likely outcome. He had taken similar steps regarding the terminations in the Fire Department for like misbehavior.

I have to say that I also had my eye on future days.

I could see that with all the strike trouble behind us, the department was going to be on an upward trajectory. Jerome Wright, a veteran police reporter for *The Commercial Appeal*, would be reporting over the next several months about signs of a new professionalism showing up in police ranks. He saw "plusses" coming out of the crisis. As did I.

A very large wound two decades in the making among fire and police personnel had been cauterized. Healing was under way.

Buddy Chapman on USSS Manley / photo Chapman Family Collection

**Buddy Chapman, second row on right
/ photo Chapman Family Collection**

Buddy Chapman / photo Chapman Family Collection

E. H. (Boss) Crump, c. 1930s
Photo courtesy of the Mississippi Valley Collection
University of Memphis, University Libraries

Beale Street in the mid-1970s
Photo courtesy of the Mississippi Valley Collection
University of Memphis, University Libraries

Buddy Chapman is sworn in by Judge Bob Love
Special Collections Department, University of Memphis

Chapman testifies to Congressional committee in Capitol
hearing room /photo courtesy Special Collections Department,
University of Memphis Libraries

Drawing by Rick Alley of The Commercial Appeal
Depicts state of police department when
Buddy Chapman was hired.

A young woman "cuffs" Chapman at banquet meeting.
Photo courtesy Special Collections Department, University
of Memphis Libraries

Buddy Chapman today.

Beale Street in recent years
Photo: Mardi Allen

7

Under a federal microscope

It was in the fall of 1978 that a unique opportunity for the Memphis Police Department first materialized.

A Dr. Fred Klyman, an associate professor with Southern Illinois University in Carbondale, called Buddy Chapman and said the school was looking for a mid-to-large police department for a partnership. He wanted to provide graduate students from the Administration of Criminal Justice program with real-world experience. Chapman replied that he would consider working with him if a path toward obtaining a degree through the university could be open to interested officers.

The deal was struck: qualified officers could follow a course of instruction leading to a Master's Degree at no cost to applicants; LEAA grant funds would be sought to pay for the program. The agreement worked well for both sides. A surprising number of officers were interested — two the first year and another 15 after that — and that made the Memphis Police Department the only police unit in the country with what essentially was an internal graduate degree program.

The deal meant that the University's computer resources were available to use for analyzing trends and evaluating progress on complex investigations. SIU students would help with analysis and shadow officers working in police management. As the program matured, officers were engaged in analyzing 500 rape cases for trends and repeat offenders. Others worked with the city's community development division to track levels of community fears and the environmental and mental factors affecting crime in seven target areas.

Police work was beginning to grow up in Memphis.

*****

A U.S. District Court suit filed in 1975 was coming to a head in early 1979. It had been filed before my time, and it alleged discrimination in police promotion practices. The lawsuit was filed by the Afro-American Police Association, a separate entity from the Memphis Police Association — one that looked out for the special interests of Black officers. The U.S. Justice Department had joined in the suit but several trial dates had been delayed as attempts were made to settle the case. The suit involved 42 officers who demanded $5 million in compensatory damages and back pay where officers might have been eligible for higher positions if a 1973 plan had been administered fairly.

Three and a half years later a settlement proposal was reached and the results seemed just and fair to me. I was eager to carry out the court's order that called for promotion of one Black police inspector, one captain, three lieutenants and five sergeants. U.S. Judge Harry Wellford also directed the parties to work toward settling a separate lawsuit concerning promotional exams that had been instituted in 1972.

That lawsuit had resulted in one of the various consent decrees under which the police department had to operate. The city said it expected agreement with the union following lifting of the restraining order.

During that same February of 1979 I was invited to appear before the U.S. Senate's Judiciary Committee. It was holding a Washington hearing on the future of the LEAA grants program. We were picked to testify because of the success of our original

108

grant of $1 million to establish the ICAP program and fund the organized crime unit.

The ICAP program highlighted for us the fact that law enforcement agencies had to work under jurisdictional boundaries while criminals did not. That led me to approach the U.S. Attorney's office for help establishing an organized crime advisory council comprised of the district attorneys and law enforcement officials from the three Mid-South states, their federal counterparts, and myself.

The invitation to Washington came as a surprise. I found myself on a bigger platform and it probably wasn't until later that I realized how rare an opportunity I was given.

I told the panel how important the LEAA funds were to our policing. I said without the funds we wouldn't have been able acquire the equipment needed to fight organized crime.

Sen. Strom Thurmond of South Carolina, presiding over the panel, asked why I couldn't get local funds to do the same thing.

"You'd wind up with councilmen haggling over one project or another," I replied. "I think it would be virtually impossible."

My testimony was well received and soon two more national invitations came my way.

It dawned on me that in the days, weeks and months following the bad publicity of the strikes, we now were being recognized as a leading department in police innovations and new-styled professionalism.

In April I was one of five people who attended a special briefing by the President's Task Force on Drug Abuse at the White House. We learned the federal drug enforcement strategy was shifting to a concentration on the trafficking of cocaine, marijuana and PCP, instead of heroin. The Memphis Police Department was chosen to be there because we had been conducting operations focusing on the very same drugs. They had become the drugs of choice among young people in Memphis and West Tennessee. We also had conducted several large drug busts in the previous three months. These Memphis police activities came to the attention of drug enforcement officials and aides in the White House.

Back in Memphis I was directing our administrative staff in revamping the testing and promotion systems following the settling of the two lawsuits brought on behalf of Black officers. We recognized we needed help in getting both done correctly so we asked the International Association of Chiefs of Police and the U.S. Justice Department to provide guidance and assistance. They gladly did.

The collaboration resulted in a new exam process by April, but it was challenged by the Memphis Police Association which claimed tests weren't "job related."

I wasn't going to relent.

I told the union that an officer's relationship with the citizens they serve, plus knowledge of what is expected of them, was at least as important as "knowing how to use a billy club." I said the test was designed for a well-rounded understanding of orders and procedures, as well as for being well-grounded in the laws in the state criminal code. The union also didn't like that I would have final approval of all promotions.

I flatly said in all ways I planned to insist on more professionalism among police officers, and I meant that. I had become used to speaking clearly to union officials. We also had drawn up best practices on agility testing for recruits and that was to be implemented for the new class rolling out in May of 1979.

Results of the new promotional exams — the first ones conducted since 1973 — came to me the morning of April 24. Our process was monitored by the federal government. The results also were mailed to the 833 officers who were required to take the test. Pursuant to promises I made, the officers who had been promoted on a temporary basis but who didn't pass the exam were returned to their previous rank.

The ones who passed the test still had to go through two more parts of the process. That consisted of a record review and a screening interview, which was conducted by three-person teams made up of a policeman, a civilian trained in personnel management and someone from an outside law enforcement agency.

The ranked list of candidates for promotion to the positions of captain and inspector came to my office. I announced my intention to promote from the ranked order on the list. I was very glad that I also could announce the list had no adverse impact on promotions for Black officers as the agreement with the Justice Department demanded.

Our new test and screening process had produced 55 candidates and 32 were Black Memphians. Until then only 16 percent of the officers were African Americans. This meant we were moving to the forefront of large city police departments in the use of new techniques to attract, hire and promote policemen and policewomen. Finally, the MPD could begin to better reflect the community it served.

Following these steps we held a very public ceremony during which Mayor Chandler and I presented the three stars of a Chief Inspector to a a deserving officer named Tom Marshal. He had been hired in 1951. He was part of the second group of Black officers hired in the city and was assigned, along with every other

Black officer, to patrol Beale Street.

Beale Street for decades reflected the heart, soul and business of Memphis. The street was lined with busy shops, theatres and cafes only two blocks from the grand Peabody Hotel.

I had promoted Marshal to acting inspector when I took the job as director. That meant he was one of the top members of the command staff and helped make policy. I found I could always rely on him in difficult situations. At the celebration that night, in his straight-forward manner, he reflected that the permanent appointment "was a long time coming." He was so right.

I have to say that there remained at that time — and up until my departure a few years after — a feeling among some of the high-ranking members of the department that final decisions on important matters only should be made by career policemen. This wrong-headed belief had existed a long time and does to this day, plaguing many American police departments.

More criticism and a great deal of grumbling occurred when I decided to reorganize the Police Training Academy and named as its leader the same Dr. Klyman who brought us the graduate degree program from Illinois. Career officers still would teach basic skills and investigative techniques. But I felt the Academy needed someone who could also see to it that officers got training in community relations and the annotated provisions of the laws. We needed an outside viewpoint from someone who was also familiar with the department.

We took a big step in community relations in June when we refined our use of deadly force policies. Several changes were needed. We redefined the actual term "dangerous felony" and elaborated at length on what the policy meant that said "all other reasonable means have been exhausted." It was too vague and widely open to interpretation. Because sometimes a person near a scene could be frightened by the arrival of police and begin to run, our new policy eliminated firing upon them unless an officer knew for certain that the person was connected to a serious crime and had been told to stop.

Use of deadly force during high-speed chases was severely limited and no officer was to fire upon anyone known to be a juvenile. Such policies should be reviewed constantly and revised as needed, and as society demands or expects.

There was a lot of behind-my-back chuckling that May when I announced that a top police official from England was coming to Memphis to conduct a series of sessions about British policing for my command staff.

I knew Geoffery James Dear, the assistant chief constable of Nottinghamshire. He was a good speaker and had conducted a condensed course on English command training all over the world. This was his first visit to an American police department. Dear was engaging and could be serious or funny as the moment required.

Plenty of skeptical members of the police brass attended his first meeting, ready to crack jokes and raise eyebrows across the aisles. Before long they were hearing facts and ideas that made them sit up and listen. At the end of the course everyone agreed the information they got was valuable. Later, Captain Don Lewis, a shift supervisor at the East Precinct station, at the Chief Constable's invitation, was chosen for a three-week tour of police departments in England to study British techniques and tactics.

My point then and now: there exist many ways and places to learn good policing. The British model that emphasizes the police force being involved with and a part of the community could be very valuable in addressing some of the problems we faced.

This visit later led to a policy of patrolmen parking their vehicles, and walking their beats one hour each shift.

8

Sitting on tenterhooks

Buddy Chapman's relationship with his boss Mayor Wyeth Chandler was a complicated one. There was mutual respect built from a long acquaintance but they never considered each other a friend. Chandler liked the fact Chapman could get things done and get them done in an orderly fashion.

Chandler was less methodical, sometimes mercurial. When he made a decision he rarely backed off. He could act rashly, or think things through carefully. It was never quite clear which of those paths he would take on any particular issue.

The Mayor usually, if in the long run, supported Chapman. He would think through an issue involving crime and the police and usually decide he needed Chapman. At the same time, he lent his ear to complaining police officers and commanders to Chapman's certain discomfort.

More than once Chandler left his police director squirming with no hint what his decision would be on an important topic. That would especially be true in the months ahead. Chandler was in a race for re-election to office. His opponents were City Councilman Pat Halloran and Otis Higgs, a former criminal court judge who had lost to Chandler in a runoff election four years earlier. Higgs had flatly stated that Chapman would be ushered out the door if he won. For his part, Chandler would not say what would happen to the police director if he remained in office.

Chapman was under a lot of pressure. Nonetheless, never a thumb-twiddler, he kept busy.

115

The major roadblocks to true reform and departmental renewal were now behind him. He had fuller control of police administration and operations. Labor strikes were history (although not forgotten). In many ways, he felt the shackles prohibiting meaningful police force change were removed.

As spring now turned to summer in 1979 he began to chip away faster at the old order — one reform at a time.

*****

In the middle of Chandler's re-election campaign, one day in July, he ordered me to stop further promotions in the ranks. The Memphis Police Association was threatening a lawsuit. At the same time, the Afro-American Police Association said it would ask the U.S. Justice Department to prevent a halt in promotions. As the parties threw word bombs, a furious Chandler changed his mind and told me to go ahead with the planned promotions. The fallout continued for two weeks but the lawsuit would ultimately fail.

July 17, 1979, started out as a calm Friday. Then stunning news came out of Washington D.C. U.S. Attorney General-Designate Benjamin Civiletti, sitting before the Senate for a confirmation hearing, announced that lawsuits were being prepared against the cities of Philadelphia, Houston and Memphis alleging a continuing history of brutality by their police departments.

Reporters soon were banging on my office door.

I really was flabbergasted by the news. I straightened my tie and explained that the last contacts I had with the Justice Department as well as the Commission on Civil Rights were very positive about steps we'd taken to halt cases of police abuse.

"I'd put Memphis' current record against any city in the nation," I said. The quote was widely used.

After answering reporters' questions I called our region's U.S.

Attorney Mike Cody. He had learned the news and had already phoned the Justice Department. He was told that although there was previous cause for concern, things in Memphis were better and that no lawsuit was contemplated against the city.

If that was true, what was Civiletti talking about?

Everyone wanted to know and I recall a long weekend wondering what had happened. Cody and *The Commercial Appeal*'s Washington Bureau reporter got to the bottom of the puzzle in their separate inquiries. Officials were definitely looking at "one city" — it later proved to be Philadelphia — and it was not Memphis. Civiletti had been handed a note that listed the three cities but his remarks at the time were in error.

As the race for mayor heated up, I decided to get some more things done. I rolled out two initiatives and they were related. Both were ideas I had discussed with Justice Department officials.

First, I reorganized the MPD's "Shoot Team" which was responsible for investigating police shootings. Second, I formed a Trial Board to hear and review administrative charges against officers.

In previous incarnations the Shoot Teams were assembled on a case-by-case basis. The new structure was permanent and headed by the police department's legal adviser who was given a small staff to investigate and keep records. The commander of the Violent Crime Investigation Division would be called on to provide additional investigators if needed and they would remain on the case, start to end.

The Trial Board was a concept for addressing serious charges against an officer that involved talks with the police union. I eliminated an old procedure where a senior commander would impose discipline and the union would appeal to me. The board was made up of five members and a simple majority vote would determine guilt or innocence.

"As director, I should not have to impose discipline on this department," I said at the time. "The police department should discipline itself."

In August of that year we experienced a shooting case that brought both initiatives into play. The incident involved the wounding by a police officer of two teenage burglary suspects at Snowden Elementary School in the Midtown area of the city.

Two officers in separate cars answered the burglary alarm. One encountered the pair as they dropped down from a low roof. He later told the Shoot Team that he was pursuing them when they turned and advanced on him. He said they ignored his orders to stop and he fired, hitting both teens. Another officer who said he was rounding a corner of the building when the shots were fired corroborated the statement.

The suspects, however, said they were running away when shot. The investigation showed that one suspect may have turned toward the officer to avoid an air conditioning unit when the patrolmen fired. The officers were relieved of duty. When the case went before the Trial Board, the officer who fired his weapon was cleared because the incident occurred in the dark in a few seconds and he could have thought the boys were moving toward him. The second officer was suspended for 20 days for lying that he witnessed the shooting in an attempt to help the other officer.

About this time I made two more changes.

One of my deputy chiefs came up with an idea — we called it Signal 12 — in which we targeted crime-troubled neighborhoods for walking patrols. For two hours every shift, 200 uniformed patrol and traffic officers were detailed to leave their marked cars in a visible location and take a walk.

I recalled that a group studying law enforcement in 1967 concluded that "the friendly cop on the beat had been replaced by a distant policeman riding in a squad car." This program broke through a barrier and new lines of communications were opened in these neighborhoods. News reports carried photos of officers talking to kids. The program had the added benefit of saving gasoline costs.

Programs like Signal 12 have come and gone over the years. They should remain in effect in all cities. Signal 12 broke down the isolation that technology causes, with the officer tied to the patrol car. One officer in 1979 told it in his own way: "You park your car and you go walking down the street and immediately everyone in the neighborhood knows you are there."

The second change was doomed from the start but I stand by it. Federal concerns and criticism from Black leaders had me thinking that I needed help breaking racial barriers. I decided to ask the Afro-American Police Association to recommend a member to work in the police department's public relations section as a liaison with Black officers. They supplied a name and I moved him from uniform patrol to PR.

The MPA hit me with a quick grievance. The two police associations held a heated meeting and the MPA announced I had violated a union contract clause prohibiting the city from negotiating with another group, union or association.

My position was I wasn't negotiating, just trying to keep a finger on the pulse and avoid new problems with the pertinent federal consent decree. But in a meeting with the Mayor and the city's personnel director I was told that technically the new post was a violation. Back on patrol went my short-lived liaison officer.

I decided I had taken one step back but three steps forward with recent initiatives to correct behaviors and improve community relations. Then a big turn the wrong way in relations happened that summer during the annual law enforcement softball championship game between the Memphis Police Department and the Shelby County Sheriff's Department at Tobey Field.

Several men drank to excess during the game that August night. Police officers who harbored bad feelings about deputies who had helped the National Guard during the police strike began to show their anger in taunts that grew ugly. That led to verbal abuse both directions around midnight, then drawn pistols and finally shots fired into the air.

I conducted a joint investigation with Sheriff Gene Barksdale. A lot of the participants wouldn't talk or said the incident was blown out of proportion. When it was over four Memphis officers were charged with rowdy behavior.

The Sheriff's team won the game. Both departments lost the match due to tarnished reputations. That was especially true for the police.

A hilarious but biting editorial cartoon showed a drunk deputy and a tipsy cop talking over a fence. In the background a gun is fired and two players are fighting with baseball bats.

The cop says to the deputy at the fence: "... Then I busted these teenage creeps for (hic) drinking and being disorderly in a public (hic) park ... Now I ask you (hic) ... what's this younger generation coming to?"

In September the city got better news out of Washington.

I flew there with City Attorney Cliff Pierce to meet with

Assistant U.S. Attorney General Drew Days who headed the Civil Rights Division in the Department of Justice. He congratulated us on improvements made in Memphis. The next day in his official report he noted my creation of a citizen police advisory board and our revision of the policy on use of deadly force. Memphis, he said, is headed in the right direction, but he added that police officers in the field now must apply the new policies.

I returned to Memphis in time to read a *Memphis Press Scimitar* investigation that brought up the issue of past police corruption. The story was a lengthy interview with a former undercover cop in the Memphis Police Department who was investigating adult clubs in the city operated by Art Baldwin. The investigation led to federal drug and tax charges and Baldwin was convicted. In the story by Kay Pittman Black the "police intelligence operative" Steve Reddish claimed that top police brass had put up roadblocks during the investigation and that dozens of police officers had taken favors from Baldwin.

The case had come to a head before I was appointed and I hadn't been informed of any internal investigation of it when I assumed the director's post. I decided to find out more. I asked for a new examination of the files. I learned from the assistant prosecutor who had tried Baldwin that he had been given a thousand-page surveillance report and that he thought federal charges could have been brought against several officers. Former Police Chief Crumby said there had been plans to bring administrative charges but admitted he didn't pass that information on to me when he left.

I spoke with a retired FBI agent. He said the case had simply fallen through cracks "because at that time the Memphis office was small" with few resources. I still wasn't satisfied. I felt I needed to quell any new reports of "widespread corruption" so I assigned a new task force to examine all files and advise me of any action that should be taken. The review turned up the names of 73 police officers who had had some contact with Baldwin, although the circumstances were murky. Of those, 12 were thought to have been involved in potential corruption activities in 1975 or early 1976. The evidence against seven seemed minor. Five may have been seriously involved but all had left the department voluntarily or had been fired.

I discussed what we found with U.S. Attorney General Cody and we decided to proceed no further.

No doubt Baldwin had a close relationship with some officers who looked the other way when illegal activities occurred in his clubs. But it was history at this point with no one interested in prosecuting. Baldwin ended up, by the way, as a government informer after a short time in prison.

One problem the Baldwin case revealed was that after a long investigation in which there was evidence of police misconduct, judicial delays could prevent taking internal personnel action. We decided to merge some functions in four squads who participated in identifying and investigating misconduct into one streamlined unit. Internal Affairs, the Security Squad, the Intelligence Squad and the Staff Inspection Squad turned the task over to the Inspectional Service Division under the command of one police inspector. It seemed that this would address practical problems such as the Baldwin case and increase police integrity by way of continuous investigation of corruption.

All that year we worked on a new program called PACE (Police And Community Enterprises) in coordination with the City of Memphis Housing and Community Development Division.

With the help of a $40,000 grant we planned to use police officers and students in the Criminal Justice Degree Program I established at Southern Illinois University to gather information in targeted depressed areas of the city. The purpose was to improve police response.

We came up with a 34-question document seeking to learn the types of crimes occurring: whether police respond effectively; how much residents spend on crime prevention such as lights, window guards or better locks; whether police understood neighborhood problems, and whether residents would move if they could. The information we received would be combined with our computerized crime data and analyzed.

I explained to the public that PACE would address community involvement in law enforcement, a fairly new concept. I have always believed that crime is a community problem, not a police problem. Police forces react and provide service in response to criminal behavior. But communities can work from within and affect criminal behaviors. I hoped PACE would provide a new understanding of neighborhood crime from the community's perspective to add to police decisions about preventive patrols. We also hoped to learn whether physical improvements in neighborhoods resulted in decreased crime.

When October came around it had been a year since the U.S. Commission on Civil Rights Southern Region had released a critical, negative assessment on police-community relations. Now Director Bobby Doctor returned to Memphis. He and Rev. Kyles, chairman of the Commission's local advisory committee, announced that our situation had jumped from a failing grade to a "C or B." We weren't to be too proud of the achievement, however, as we were informed a great deal of work remained to be done. Doctor recognized my efforts but said in some cases my actions had been reversed or undermined by Mayor Chandler.

"We feel that the Director has not received the support he should," Doctor said. "This gives police officers in this city aid and comfort in knowing that when they get out in the streets and violate department rules they can find a way to be bailed out.

"We also have contended for a long time that there has not been enough involvement by the city council."

Doctor wasn't finished. He then took to task news media executives and religious leaders. He said news bosses had the attitude that they only report the news not make it, and that the Memphis Ministers Association believe that as a group they shouldn't be involved in police-community relations.

On the other hand, he reported that business leaders responded to the Commission more favorably. "They realize that bad police-community relations drives away industry. But the problem is the responsibility of the entire community, not just Director Chapman's."

Looking back, I find it interesting that this came at a time when I had no idea what the future held for me as director of police. I didn't know if I retained Mayor Chandler's support.

There still were plenty of officers in the ranks who disliked me, felt I wasn't one of them, and hoped I'd soon disappear. The police association had a specific goal of giving me the boot. Chandler's opponents were approached and promised union support if they would agree to replace me with a career policeman. Union president David Baker was routinely quoted in the newspapers blaming me for morale problems and a discipline lapse. In one story he said, "The police department is in a miserable state of affairs and will remain that way until Police

Director E. Winslow Chapman is replaced."

Press-Scimitar Editor Milton Britten carried a leading editorial in the afternoon paper late in October that was entitled "Trouble in the Ranks." It was succinct. It opined that low morale and disciplinary problems had been no secret.

"Nor do Memphians get much comfort from such recent actions on the part of their law enforcers as the softball game where off-duty officers were drinking beer illegally in a city park, and shots were fired in a parking lot. Or the party for new recruits, which featured a pool dunking and fisticuffs. Or the case of an officer releasing two gambling suspects to protect a vice squad officer's insistence on arresting another man the first officer thought should go free. Or the case where a policeman neglected to report shots fired at fleeing burglary suspects, one of whom later turned up wounded."

The editorial then listed what it said were my good ideas to boost morale: "including voluntary rotating shifts, choice assignments for officers who do a good job, merit pay to reward dedication to police work, better pay for commanders, and more visits in the field to determine officers' needs."

In truth, I did have plenty of supporters in the community and those were measures I promoted. And, to complete the picture about my visits in the field: yes I wanted to know what officers needed. I also wanted them to be aware that they never could be sure when I might show up and see exactly what they were up to.

Reporter Jerome Wright with *The Commercial Appeal* wrote a news analysis a month later that pulled back all the covers. His story began: "Depending on whom you talk to within the police department, Police Director E. Winslow Chapman is either an egotistical despot or a man who has done a great deal to move the department forward." His story depicted me as a "hip-shooting, 37-year-old" and the most controversial of Chandler's division directors — "the one Chandler apparently has the hardest time keeping in line."

By now, the mayoral race had become a two-man contest, with only Higgs left to prevent Chandler from a third term of office. Election Day came and Chandler won. Still I didn't know what the future held. The Mayor had never given a clear statement of what he would do with me even when I had become a major issue in the campaign. Now he was taking his good time deciding whether I would stay or go. Reporter Wright was correct in further describing me as confused and a bit worried.

Wright quoted me as saying that the main problem I had was that many of the rank and file police "didn't understand or accept my position of not tolerating wrongdoing. They feel that they can undercut anything I do by running to the Mayor."

I felt then and still do now, that this was an accurate criticism. The Mayor allowed, even encouraged people to go around channels and straight to him. He liked being in the know that way and didn't pay attention to the chaos it could create.

Chandler was a brilliant public official, but one never knew for certain what he was thinking. I'm convinced he liked it that way.

I put my head down and kept doing what I had done. I continued looking for ways to become a better police director. I attended training courses, including one at the FBI Academy and another at the Regional Organized Crime Information Center. When our Integrated Criminal Apprehension Program (ICAP) of computerized crime data got national attention, I consulted and lectured in several cities.

One day late in the year Cliff Pierce and I were called back to Washington to follow up with a new report on our efforts to improve police-community relations. Justice Department officials had expressed interest in our revised shooting policy and the fact we now included community relations and proper use of deadly force in our training of police recruits, so I took Shoot Team commander Clyde Keenan and the director of the training academy, Fred Klyman with me to the nation's capital. We met with Days and his staff for several hours this time and we were a hit when describing our "shoot / don't shoot" training video.

Part of yearly firearms training involved a police officer wearing headphones and a simulation firearm in a holster. Officers are shown various situations on a video screen and must react quickly. I remember trying it myself several times. I never did score well.

Just like other big city police departments, we had been using a canned video format available commercially. But when I tried the simulation I could see that the various scenarios on screen didn't relate to Memphis reality. There were too many scenarios involving clusters of high-rise buildings. The scenarios we needed would depict neighborhoods, convenience stores or strip malls.

We decided to create our own training video. I formed a team from the command staff to review apropos incidents —from not too serious to the deadly encounters to be avoided at all cost. We used federal grant funds designated for police training and got the film done.

Dr. Klyman's review of recruit training techniques also scored with the Justice Department and led to them becoming models for other departments.

If I sound proud, well, I am.

Back in town, the Mayor announced his decision to reappoint all current division directors — except me. Said the Mayor: "The fact that Director Chapman is being singled out for a more lengthy assessment should not be taken to mean anything more than the fact that the nature of his position has created more public interest than any other Director." He said he knew there were strong feelings about me, pro and con, in the community. He admitted that the most vocal critics were in the police department and especially in the union and that I had wide and growing support in the Black community.

He didn't specify anyone who was opposed, including his two veteran police bodyguards who were his constant companions.

The Commercial Appeal's reporter Tom Jordan decided to gauge the pros and the cons mentioned by Chandler. In an article he quoted an informed source who revealed that the Mayor had received more than 40 letters, dozens of phone calls and even people "who had come in off the street" to voice support of keeping me as director. It seemed that support throughout the city outweighed the assault by Chief Crumby holdouts.

It was on a cold day in December when Chandler announced that he would re-nominate me to the city council to continue to serve. The choicest quote I recall concerning this time came from Henry Evans. Henry was the city's chief administrative officer, a personal friend and one of the biggest supporters of my efforts to reform the Memphis Police Department. He called me "first in our hearts and last to be reappointed."

The truth is, police reform is hard and often thankless. Serious reformers must grow thick skin or find other ways to occupy their time.

9

Back to the bargaining bench

It had been less than two years since the police strike and it was time for new talks with Memphis Police union representatives. Besides wages the biggest question came down to who had final say in disciplining officers who broke regulations and the law.

Everyone knew misconduct problems persisted.

They ranged from police brutality to outright acts of disobedience and covert misdeeds that stemmed from ignorance or prejudice. One or both was behind an officer's plan as he made his way to a workroom and switched on a photocopy machine one day when he was alone. He had a small flyer that contained insults to people of color, not his color, which was white. It was the stuff of Jim Crow days. Of small minds and smaller motivations.

His plan was simple. Make copies and pass them around to like-minded comrades. He didn't know the days when an act like his might be overlooked and bring knowing chuckles were already over. He didn't realize he now was part of a police force that no longer would tolerate racism in its ranks. It really was a new day. He just hadn't been listening.

******

It is a rare day indeed when the leader of a major urban police department can say "Not much happened today." I had very few such days. There was always a problem. Some were big problems. Some were bigger than big. Many involved my up-to-now tenuous relationship with the police association.

I found out one morning in January of 1980 that an officer had used a police copy machine to duplicate inflammatory literature about Blacks and passed it around to white officers. The material clearly was derogatory and racist. A member of the Afro-American Police Officers Association obtained some of the material and brought it to my attention.

I learned that a lieutenant was aware of the officer's action but had taken no steps to stop it. He was charged with neglect of duty and suspended for 15 days without pay. The officer who distributed the materials faced termination. He chose to resign instead.

During the disciplinary hearing a new Memphis Police Association president sat in. Ray Maples would prove to be a constant breath of fresh air after his predecessor's term. Maples said he realized the gravity of the offense and the impact it could have on the MPA which cared to represent all officers. He didn't challenge the outcome.

On another day I learned that a gun had been discharged into the ceiling of the North Precinct break room during an after-hours pool game that turned ugly. There was a fight and five police officers were present. The quintet refused to answer investigators' questions so all five policemen were fired.

In this case Maples declared the dismissals were wrong and we were "trying to force statements under duress." I pointed out the union's contract with the city was perfectly clear: officers are required to give statements in investigative hearings. After two hours of discussion, Maples suggested a compromise. The officer who fired the shot and a second involved in the altercation would be dismissed; the other three would be reinstated with a five-day suspension. He said the three thought they were being accused but were only witnesses. Now they were willing to give complete statements. I accepted this as a fair outcome, hardly covering my surprise at the proffered compromise.

New negotiations with the MPA were scheduled to start in a week's time. I began to relax just a bit about the prospects of reaching a new contract.

Another incident occurred right after that hearing that prompted a quick response from me. A five-year veteran patrolman encountered a couple in a car one night. He handcuffed the man, locked him in the patrol car, and raped the woman. Physical evidence confirmed the couples' statements. He was terminated at an administrative hearing and left to face the criminal charge of rape. The union appealed but when they learned the officer was outside his assigned territory and that just getting into the car with the woman was a terminating offense, the union pursued it no further.

During this time we had been investigating a patrolman for possible drug trafficking. We had planned to catch him in a large delivery but he was tipped off. It was obvious that someone in the Narcotics Division let him know about the sting. I had been concerned about a long-standing practice called "bidding assignments" in which command level jobs were awarded based on seniority only. I was resolved to address this during negotiations in sensitive areas such as narcotics and intelligence squads. Meanwhile we determined we had ample evidence against the patrolman without catching him red-handed in a sting and he was fired.

The meetings over a new contract began in February. Even though I was feeling comfortable in my dealings so far with Maples, I wasn't looking forward to negotiations. This would be the first talk over a new contract since the damaging fire and police strikes. Emotional wounds from that experience still festered on both sides and in the community at large.

The contract was set to expire in April and both sides doubted a new agreement could be reached by that time. The framework for the talks did show promise. For one thing, the news media was invited to witness the negotiations. For another, a new set of rules was designed to prevent a stalemate leading to a strike. If an agreement couldn't be reached on economic items, a three-member committee made up of city council members would take charge and recommend an offer to the full council. If the whole council rejected the committee's recommendation, the last and best offer would become effective. It was very complicated but at least seemed to aim toward a final determination.

Les Real, newly appointed manager of labor relations, was the chief negotiator for the city. He and I would sit on one side of the table. Maples designated the union's attorney Ted Hansom as their lead. The sides would find themselves far apart on the wages front although that wouldn't be discussed until well into the talks. The city's first offer was a 9.4 percent wage increase. The union asked for a 23 percent hike. But there were many other issues to wrestle over before the money was broached.

The MPA wanted a career development plan to prevent officers from feeling stale on the job. Our answer to this was a new in-service training program we had been designing.

State law required 40 hours of training for all law enforcement officers each year. Any officer who didn't pass the course lost a $600 pay supplement. In the past this system had been something of a joke with officers, who passed the course regardless of how they performed on tests. Our new program was built around elective courses meant to match an officer's development ambitions. And every officer would genuinely have to pass to earn the bonus pay and be eligible for a new posting,

Courses were to be offered in general investigative techniques, helping patrolmen become eligible for promotion to sergeant; first-line supervision, so that sergeants and patrol officers could be eligible for promotion to lieutenant positions, and patrol techniques, for patrol officers with less than five years experience. Captains and lieutenants, who weren't covered by the bargaining unit, already had a four-hour monthly management development course they attended during their regular tours of duty. All courses were intended to serve as a first phase of a four-step promotional procedure.

We shared this plan with the U.S. Justice Department. They approved it and were interested in our sharing it across the nation once it was fully in place. This proposal proved to be a quick and successful item in talks with the union. By March about a dozen issues had reached tentative approval by both sides. Remaining issues would prove more complicated. The sides were miles apart on language surrounding job bidding, internal investigations and disciplinary measures.

News stories prompted a strongly worded editorial in the morning newspaper. Its headline declared "The Right To Manage." The opinion piece cataloged a litany of both historic and recent examples of serious police misconduct. The editorial stated, "The fact that the MPA was able to overturn a number of disciplinary actions ordered by Police Director E. Winslow Chapman following the 1978 strike suggests that too much power was given the union in this area in the last contract." It concluded that city managers must save the right to manage.

It was well understood that the union's so-called "absolute" positions in these area would later serve as bargaining chips when it was time to discuss wages.

When our side brought up the need to do background checks when an officer bid for a posting in Narcotics or Intelligence, the union side refused to discuss the matter. When I said we would discuss the matter or I would disband the Narcotics unit and turn over narcotics enforcement to the Sheriff's office, the union team stormed from the session. As they stood to go they declared they wouldn't be threatened where the rights of members were concerned. I said back (we were shouting by then) I had to have implicit trust in those leading drugs investigations.

There followed a lengthy absence from the bargaining table, with incriminations going on outside the talks. Finally their team returned, agreeing to discuss a set of requirements beyond simple seniority. I later learned that during the break in talks there were internal union arguments over whether I meant what I said. Some believed I would never agree to give up power over narcotics investigations. But as one person reportedly said, "We'd better be careful. That crazy son of a bitch might really do it."

Of course, I don't identify my confidential sources.

Once we had agreed on language on various non-economic issues — with the exception of internal investigations and discipline — we started to talk about money matters. Before even getting to basic hourly wages, we had two other big costs to discuss. One was court time and the other was overtime. Both had a tremendous impact on the city's budget.

Because a policeman or policewoman is required by law to be present in court for cases they worked, he or she was paid an automatic four hours whether they participated in proceedings or not, plus any full hour above four they had to stay. Additionally, officers were paid overtime when needed by the department or when required to stay involved in a situation such as a traffic accident. The union disputed the point, but the vast majority of officers were paid overtime each week.

The policy in effect then was that overtime rates applied after 48 hours of work in a week. The union proposed changing that to time over 40 hours. The proposal by itself would have cost the city about $1 million then. The city rejected that but said our side would concede to 40 hours in exchange for a smaller minimum for court appearances. We pointed out that the amount of hours paid was considerably more than officers actually worked in court settings. To be more fully on top of final costs, each side then brought in its initial offer on wages and as expected we were far apart.

As the sides again addressed the twin entrenched issues of internal investigations of misconduct and disciplinary procedures, the union raised an important point showing the overlap between economic and non-economic articles in the discussions. The union's chief negotiator said that in previous contracts the city had agreed to latitude in disciplinary areas in exchange for wage agreements favorable to the city. While he was right, I insisted I was responsible to the whole community and to good officers for holding bad officers accountable for unacceptable behaviors.

The union agreed with me on that but they wanted the ordinary rights of officers protected. We soon realized that the real issue was the use of the Trial Board I had set up — the selection of officers to serve on the board, evidentiary rules at the hearings, and the procedure for suspending officers. We all realized that each side had important needs and fair considerations. After exhaustive

135

conversations, we reached a tentative agreement on new internal investigative procedures.

Tom Jordan's story in the next day's newspaper explained well the accord we reached. For one thing, both sides agreed that an officer would not be disciplined merely for refusing to take a lie detector test. The union in turn agreed to drop a section in the contract that would warn citizen complainants that they were liable for making false statements about a police officer. New procedures were set in place for internal investigations and the specific rights of officers were established.

Jordan wrote that the agreed language was a "very significant movement" toward a new contract. That was exactly what we all thought. A few days later, on March 17, the bargainers continued to talk about disciplinary procedures. Although close to a final agreement on the issue, a new obstacle developed.

I claimed a police director had the right to order reassignment of an officer for disciplinary reasons. The union called that an "extreme form of punishment just short of termination." This led to numerous caucus meetings, after which the union advanced new language about a temporary transfer of an individual following a disciplinary hearing. I told our chief negotiator to stand fast on the issue and so it was put off for later review.

At this point we were at the start of April with two weeks left in the time set for reaching an agreement. We were at an impasse on discipline and seniority-only job bidding, and wages were still 14 percentage points apart. Talking about the issues became hard and the words we used grew tougher.

Ted Hansom for the union warned the city against trying to "buy back" control of issues relinquished in past years when the city had little money to offer. "They are not for sale at any price," he said.

I said at a meeting on April 2 that I wasn't just trying to regain lost control. "I absolutely intend to get it back …Just because you have had something you never should have been given does not mean you are still going to get it."

The union then turned to wages, tying it to the current Consumer Price Index plus 6 percent. At that time, the net increase would have been 18.5 percent under the proposal, but unknown after that first year. The city rejected the new offer. We now were counting the days to a possible walkout or strike.

On April 9 we settled on how to resolve the issue of transferring an officer "for cause." The director could transfer a problem officer for a three-month cooling off period after which he would return to his previous assignment. If a problem recurred, a hearing would be held to determine if the officer or his supervisor was the source of the problem.

If trouble persisted the union would attempt to get the officer to voluntarily transfer. If he refused he would be subject to disciplinary action, including being fired.

This worked for both sides. Now we talked about the issue of bidding for a job with only seniority considered. I told the union that a recent problem in the Intelligence Squad showed what was wrong with the system. The 12 members in Intelligence — made up of some of the most senior people in the whole department — had stopped functioning effectively. The only way out under the old contract was for me to disband the unit.

Our senior negotiator further pointed out that under the system a younger person in the police department was stymied. "No matter how well you do, until you have at least 10 years of experience no avenues are open to you," he said. That described quite a few younger officers.

The union caucused, then asked that we outline a new review process to be used to evaluate officers bidding for positions in Intelligence, Vice and Narcotics divisions. We did and the union accepted the process.

On Monday evening, April 14, 1980 — the final day in the contract negotiations — union members voted overwhelmingly in favor of a new contract. Police would receive a 17.75 percent increase over the course of two years and the Director of Police would regain control over procedures, discipline and other matters lost in previous bargaining. Both sides got a lot of what they wanted. Firefighters and the AFSCME members followed soon thereafter in reaching their own bargains with the City.

"Who won?" asked *The Commercial Appeal* in an editorial.

"The public," was its own answer to the question.

It was one week later that word came of other news, one worthy of celebration by the entire community, and one that represented a victory in my efforts to achieve meaningful change in the police force. The news first came over the UPI and AP wire services. The U.S. Department of Justice announced a "sweeping and unprecedented" agreement with the City of Memphis and Memphis Police, taking the city out from under a federal oversight and consent decree. We were back in charge of investigating misconduct and the use of deadly force on our own without federal scrutiny.

This was the result of all the meetings at "Main Justice" offices, all our efforts to comply and to show the Civil Rights Division that we meant to bring about change. I spoke later with Asst. Attorney General Days. He told me that besides the concrete steps we had taken to address issues, I had consistently demonstrated sincerity and that had altered the federal government's low perception of the city. I told him the work of Henry Evans, Cliff Pierce and others was invaluable.

Unusually tall headlines hit the front pages detailing the settlement on how we would address deadly force and other issues in the city. I signed the agreement as soon as it reached my desk.

In Philadelphia the outcome was different. City officials there had denied charges of racial discrimination in their practices and refused to negotiate with Justice officials. The government filed suit against the city. That suit was dismissed by a federal judge but the Justice Department appealed. That city would finally reach an accord more than a year later.

It also was at this time that the investigation into drug dealing within the MPD's Narcotics Division concluded. Five patrolmen were named in federal indictments. Two of them already had resigned. The other three had been suspended until the outcome of the investigation. Now they were terminated.

The officers had been providing protection to a major drug dealer. They picked up drugs for him and transported them to the dealer's sub-dealers around the city. They also were shown to have lied to police and a federal grand jury. They went on to be prosecuted in U.S. District Court.

I stated publicly that the case disproved a contention that a law enforcement agency was incapable of policing itself. I also knew the point was emphatically made to the rank and file that a time of looking the other way when fellow officers were involved in illegal activities was over.

The month of June arrived and brought more good news. We reached an agreement with the MPA on procedures for promotions and a lawsuit that had been in limbo during negotiations was withdrawn. The union had learned that the federal government was inclined to think that too much weight on seniority would adversely affect black officers' chances for promotion.

Days later, on June 10, I promoted 25 white and 11 black officers to the rank of sergeant. This was a big deal for me as well as for them. Those promotions put us in compliance with another federal consent decree governing promotion of African Americans in proportion to their number.

I have to admit I was riding mighty high at this time, with so many things going our way, and positive, long-lasting changes occurring in the department. It's times like that, of course, when fate likes to step in and put you on a quick descent back to earth.

It came with a critical headline: "Man Dies of Injuries After Fight With Officers." All the consent decrees roared back in my mind. The specter of possible police brutality loomed before me. The officers were white and the victim was black so civil rights violations were possible as well.

The news also brought to mind the earlier killing of a black teenager named Elton Hays. The circumstances of that boy's death in 1971 sound all too familiar all these years later (including recent national cases such as the murder by Derek Chauvin of George Floyd or the beating and death in Memphis of Tyre Nichols).

Hays fled from police after a traffic stop but was apprehended in the county by Sheriff's deputies, who beat him severely before turning him over to city police. The policemen in turn beat him some more. By the time he was taken to a hospital he was dead, the victim of a savage "we'll teach you a lesson" kind of hypocrisy. Did we have such an occurrence again late that summer of 1980?

The new incident began the night of September 18 with a call to police from relatives of William Lee Hoskins, 29, in the Dixie Homes housing project near downtown. They said he had a mental condition, had been drinking and was "acting wild." Two officers arrived and as they talked to the man's mother and sister, Hoskins rushed outside and began struggling with the officers. Witnesses agreed that as the officers attempted to subdue Hoskins he broke free and fled, the officers in hot pursuit through the project's acres of yards, sidewalks and parking slots.

In later statements, the officers said they caught up with Hoskins and a second struggle among the three ensued. They said Hoskins maneuvered on top of one patrolman and went for his gun. The second officer pulled him away and as he tugged he said he struck Hoskins three times with his flashlight in order to subdue him. The third blow rendered the man unconscious and he later died. The officers' statements weren't corroborated by some of the neighborhood witnesses. Some said Hoskins had ceased running, tried to surrender when the two officers both beat him with their flashlights. Some said he was lying on the ground, face down, and wasn't resisting arrest.

Soon enough, community activists sounded alarms. Reporters pressed for more information.

The Shelby County Medical Examiner was Dr. Jerry Francisco at the time. He conducted an autopsy on Hoskins' body. In his report he ruled that the victim had received three blows from a heavy object and the last was fatal, in part because of the large quantity of medications mixed with alcohol in his system.

Francisco further stated he found blood only on one flashlight. All of the pertinent facts in the report were consistent with the officers' statements. Francisco added that there was evidence of other blows and they appeared to come from fists. That was consistent with the first struggle. I ordered police to re-examine witnesses and hunt for new people who may have seen the arrest. More statements came in, including one from a state senator. But some of the statements were made by people our investigation showed couldn't have observed what they reported. One person even claimed the officers had tied Hoskins to a tree before assaulting him. The two officers had been on patrol in the area for some months. Their records didn't reveal a single complaint or allegation of misconduct.

Black community leaders refused to accept the medical examiner's findings. At the very least, they said, too much force was used in the incident. They demanded Francisco's removal from the case and announced an independent investigation. They enlisted the help from the national office of the NAACP. A lawyer for the family even suggested the there would be a demand for the body's exhumation for more pathological study.

Black members of the Shelby County Commission asked the Sheriff to conduct an independent investigation. We supplied all our evidence. When that probe was completed it concurred with the police findings. The Sheriff's examination did turn up the additional fact that the holster worn by the officer overcome by Hoskins had been torn, evidence that Hoskins had tried to get his gun.

A forensic pathologist from Atlanta, Dr. Robert Stivers, was hired to review Francisco's findings. His report concurred with the initial forensic study's conclusion.

Reporters asked me for comments. I said I would welcome any further probe by any legitimate group and suggested the possibility that a grand jury be convened to review the facts. On

142

December 9 a grand jury was convened by the Shelby County District Attorney General's office. The jury reviewed all evidence assembled by the various parties to date. That jury refused to issue an indictment.

In the end the charge of a cover-up didn't apply in this particular case. But it must be said that the potential for believing in one is always just beneath the surface in most cities, especially as long as suspicion persists of the rank and file or of law enforcement leaders and other public officials. Skepticism of official accounts in such cases will remain as long as the questionable use of deadly force — or abuse of suspects based on race — continues to happen anywhere in the country.

10

Under the gun

The church's sanctuary was crowded. Pews were filled and latecomers found folding chairs hastily placed in the outside aisles, near the windows. The police director was introduced. He stood at the pulpit, just a few feet away from the first row of angry and concerned citizens. He could see in their faces how much they wanted answers.

Several reporters stood at the back, ready to scribble his comments.

What would he say about the crime spree in the city, a "crime cloud" as the Director had called it and that hadn't skipped their neighborhood?

What was he going to do about the rise in aggravated assaults, armed robberies, burglaries and thefts, murders and rapes? Did he understand their fears, their frustrations?

Why couldn't he get more done?

What could they as citizens do about the problem besides organize a watch program? Would he send more patrols? Could he help streamline the court system? What about hiring more police officers to hunt down more crooks?

What the hell are you going to do, Director Chapman?

******

The result of our first PACE survey arrived on my desk late in 1980. Information had been gathered all year in seven target neighborhoods chosen based on crime statistics. The project took citizen perceptions about crime and police response and overlaid those with crime data for a unique perspective.

I was keen to see what people said. There were some surprises.

The areas we studied were predominantly Black (97 percent). Yet the residents in all the neighborhoods gave police good grades for addressing crime, a rate of 64 percent. When asked if police understood problems in their communities, 74 percent responded affirmatively.

Respondents identified burglary as the biggest crime problem (84 percent) followed by armed robbery (28 percent). (Of course, guns weren't as ubiquitous then as they are today.) Asked if they felt safe where they lived, 78 percent did during daylight hours but only 37 percent felt safe at night.

Nearly half of the respondents said they would move if they could. I found it interesting that the neighborhoods with the highest crime rates gave the highest grades to police. The survey indicated that people realized they have a part to play in crime prevention and 88 percent of them said they would report suspicious activity.

Although the results from our PACE questionnaire were somewhat fascinating, they really pointed us nowhere. What could we do with the data? We decided this was a good exercise but a bit too time-consuming and not worth repeating.

Good managers know that is how it is sometimes. Ideas come from people who have them. Some people get lots of ideas. The ideas might prove useful or might prove to have less-than-exciting results. Some ideas even prove to have been a bit crazy.

What's important is to have them, invite them and test them. It's sometimes good to just try an idea on for size. Then you need people around you that you trust to tell you if it works or if it was one of those crazy ideas. If a project is going nowhere, accept the fact and move on. That's what we did in this case.

I am sure those survey statistics wouldn't hold up today. The reasons are complicated. But in 1980 we at least could see the spectrum of community feelings.

At one end there were too many cops who harbored an "us against them" attitude and who felt most people didn't understand the nature of their work. At the other end were activists who said they believed police are inherently cruel and brutal, particularly in the treatment of Blacks, and that the cruelty arises from prejudice and a mentality that seeks to cover up wrongdoing. In the wide middle were people trying to live their lives in peace and security and who relied on police to react as needed.

The nature of the problem was clear. The answers always have been harder to define and carry out.

I do know this: the vast majority of police officers complete their careers without complaints or charges on their record. This includes those who were required to resort to the use of physical force at some point and even those who had to use deadly force.

Other statistics late that year seemed to show we were making improvements in insisting that the police department "police" itself.

In 1977 a record number of brutality complaints were filed — 411. That number fell to 303 in 1978 and further slipped to 277 in 1979. The numbers (still too high) dropped another 24 in 1980. We released a report on the numbers. Maxine Smith, who led the Memphis Branch of the NAACP, took issue with it. Reports to her office hadn't declined, she said. As I have written, I had deep respect for her and wanted to know if she was right. I called on Captain William Mosely for help.

I appointed Mosely as the first Black officer to head the Internal Affairs Division of the force in 1978. First, though, we had several in-depth conversations. He knew how I felt about any officer mistreating a citizen. He wanted to make sure he could count on my support. I wanted him to review the current function of Internal Affairs but to also seek input from the Black community.

He did and the information he obtained along with his own observations led to fundamental changes. He had noted that many people were intimidated when they came to police headquarters to make a complaint, so we decided to rent business space in a nearby office building. Mosely also wanted to be involved in the selection of his officers and he wanted them to have diverse backgrounds. I agreed to that, too. We obviously had similar ideas about what was needed in that division of the police.

His final suggestion was that his officers should work in business attire — "no guns or badges showing." I said fine. In a later meeting, he said that many people walking in with complaints thought they were talking to civilian employees of the police, not actual officers. It worked.

So I asked Mosely to help me understand the discrepancy between our complaints and Maxine Smith's experience. He said that our numbers were right and that she was right as well. He explained that some people who complained to the NAACP were unwilling to make formal complaints to Internal Affairs. A formal written complaint is required by law for a legal investigation of police actions to proceed.

I had a follow-up conversation with Smith. "I am tired of people trying to protect the police force when they should be protecting us," she said. "For every officer Mosely and his squad investigate and find guilty of infractions, there are probably 10 that are valid but he doesn't get."

Then she relented in one respect. "At least one benefit to the Black community has come of the police effort to stop brutality by its officers. There aren't as many of us getting killed by policemen now."

That was hyperbole, perhaps, but her point was well taken.

Meanwhile, I was announcing other changes to the public at nightly community meetings and through the press about reducing response time and centralizing telephone complaints and inquiries.

The average time it took from when an officer got a call to arrival on a scene was seven and a half minutes. We wanted to achieve an average of five minutes. We planned to do this by requiring tighter monitoring of calls by supervisors and by using the Integrated Crime Analysis computer system for a more efficient deployment of patrols and manpower.

Our police operators handled any call that came in — requests for information, complaints or reports of crimes. There was no priority ranking. So we proposed three separate numbers. One for serious calls needing immediate response, one for general information and one for document requests. The latter two blended at night during the peak time for critical calls for help.

This of course was before the age of 9-1-1 systems. But it did streamline our call center and help us with our response times.

Throughout the country crime was on a steep upward curve. "America is afraid," said a story about national crime data in the *Press-Scimitar*. The Memphis crime stats for 1980 were released in January of 1981 and felony crime increases were dramatic almost across the board, reversing a four-year downward trend. There were record numbers in rape, robbery and assaults. Homicides missed reaching a record by only one murder and had gone up 41 percent over the previous year.

The revelations caused a lot of concern and conversation in the community about repeat offenders, the need for a tougher response in the judicial and correctional systems, and the need to add police officers. If the city was sitting on a hot stove, the pan of collective emotions was a boil. This was when I made a speech to a neighborhood group and one comment that came out of my feverish brain became a verbal explosion like fireworks that just won't stop igniting in a warehouse fire.

Today we would say my words went viral.

One type of violent crime that had hiked in big numbers in Memphis was rape and sexual assault, at least in the number of reports of the crime. In some corners, Memphis was called the "rape capital of the nation."

American society was rapidly going through changes in the treatment of certain crimes against women, including sexual assaults and domestic violence, or what at the time was usually called "wife beating" or spouse battering. Change was long overdue.

A number of women's advocacy groups had worked with me to form a Rape Crisis Center. They easily persuaded me that it was a crucially needed service. But opening the Center was only a first step. I was surprised to learn soon after that the Center's director was accusing police of callous treatment of rape victims. I looked into the problem and found a long list of misunderstandings. Some were the fault of the police.

One victim and her family were told that the Center was closed at night. It was, but they weren't explained the alternative. Officers needed to tell victims that advocates were available by phone and were supposed to respond to an officer's call. Another problem arose when a family was

148

told it couldn't accompany a victim to the Center after an attack. It turned out the investigator said one companion could go but not all five members of the family.

I directed the commander of the Violent Crime Squad to work through the communication problems and make sure police were knowledgeable and would fully and with compassion inform families of procedures when they were going through such tragic circumstances. Despite the initial hiccups, things did improve. But Memphis and the rest of the nation had a long way to go in the investigation and humane response to women's reports of abuse.

As some rape cases got close public scrutiny and as I found myself speaking about the crime increases more and more, one evening I uttered the infamous line that was a proverbial shot heard around the globe. The quote probably brought me more press coverage and public attention — good, bad and neutral — than anything else I did or said in my time as police director.

The setting was an evening meeting held in a church and sponsored by the Vollintine-Evergreen Community Association. As many as 200 concerned citizens were present that night. I spoke and then took questions. It went on for 90 minutes. When asked what should be done about criminals like rapists, I said in part, "This may shock some of you but if maybe we could castrate rapists one or two times ... that crime would go down the drain. I'm convinced of that." I also mentioned more executions of murderers.

Some people looked shocked. Many nodded their heads. A few yelled out "Yeah!" and "Yes sir!" As the evening wound down, I came back to that concept and elaborated on my meaning.

"Although America isn't ready for mutilation and corporal punishment of that sort — society would consider that inhumane — it's important to realize that rapists feel they can get away with the crime. There are too many repeat rapists."

Naturally, it was the first line that was remembered and repeated and published in news stories. To understand the effects of the statement, just read a few headlines that appeared over the next several days above news articles and opinion columns:

'Bizarre' Punishment Fits Rapist, Chapman Declares
Chapman: Castrate Rapists And Electrocute Murderers
Some Laud, Some Rap Chapman's Statements
Castration Comment Attracts U.S. Attention to Chapman
National Attention Focused On Comments by Chapman
Justice East of The Mississippi?
No Need To Be Stingy With Castrations And Sizzlings

My phone would not stop ringing. The local newspapers published dozens of letters from readers.

"Underneath this captivating exterior is a man who rises to the occasion no matter the task," wrote one admiringly.

"Chapman's statements show who the real political opportunist is," wrote another appalled citizen.

One letter below the headline, "Cool it" said, "Your suggestion to castrate rapists and sizzle murderers as deterrents to crime is inflammatory and counterproductive."

Two leading community leaders gave their opinions. A C Wharton, the county's public defender and a future mayor of both the county and the city, dismissed the notion of castration. He was speaking to the Shelby County Republican Women's Club for the express purpose of rebutting my remarks. He said he was "flabbergasted" by what I said. The energy I spent on venting frustrations, he said, could be better spent on constructive solutions.

Civil rights attorney D'Army Bailey wrote a guest column in *The Commercial Appeal* that had a slightly different take:

"At times a wild and inflammatory idea can be beneficial in the long run by helping to bring about greater public understanding of an issue. Such is the case with Police Director E. Winslow Chapman's suggestion that the state ought to castrate rapists and 'sizzle' murderers." But, he concluded, "Memphis is not that kind of vicious community."

All over the city, and indeed throughout the nation, people were discussing and arguing over my remark. In London, *The Globe* ran a story and a photo of me. Beneath a brief headline "**Castrate Rapists**," the article began, "One of President Reagan's top police advisers says rapists should be castrated to halt the alarming rise in rape cases."

All these decades later I do not regret the remark.

Was I using hyperbole to highlight a real problem and the frustrations felt over finding solutions? Of course. Was I aware of how much reaction there would be? Of course not.

I was trying, probably not as effectively as I would have liked, to address what I saw then and still see now as two dangerous lines of thought about crime.

The first is that crime is out of control and we can do nothing about it. A community can cut crime if it seriously means to. It can prevent crime by not accepting it and coming together. In the case of rape, I had once coined a term that I called "recreational rapist." I was convinced then and still am that the vast majority of rapists aren't pathological or mentally deranged. They are mean, vicious individuals who enjoy hurting and subjugating others. They enjoy the control they experience in rape. Also, because too many rapes are never reported, many rapists think there won't be consequences.

The second line of dangerous thinking is that the one and only answer to crime is to pour more police onto the streets. That too is wrong. Police react to circumstances. They prevent only by being in the right place at the right time, or to whatever degree criminals fear being caught. It is true that there were then and are now police shortages that must be addressed. But more cops do not equal fewer crimes. The equation isn't mathematical or scientific.

The Commercial Appeal and *Memphis Press-Scimitar* addressed the issue in editorials as it swirled and bubbled over.

"Overlooking the director's excesses, one finds some of his comments right on the button," the *Press-Scimitar* editorial said. It went on, "Chapman's back obviously was to the wall Sunday when he faced 200 or so citizens concerned about crime … But the citizens' backs also are to the wall. They are scared. And they need sound, realistic, practical anti-crime advice from their top police official much more than they need unrealistic, impractical frustration-venting."

"Swaggering rhetoric can sound good — even just —but it won't make women any safer in Memphis, and that's what needs to be done," chimed *The Commercial Appeal.*

I accepted those criticisms then and still do today.

The castration remark probably was one of those "hip shots" Jerome Wright said I could tend toward when under the gun, so to speak. More than once at that time, a rapist had been caught, released on a low bond, and then found to rape again. The whole community was frustrated, myself included.

What I meant that night simply was, enough is enough.

But I also know that those words would have been quickly forgotten. There might have been one or two brief news accounts of my remarks that night and then the news media would move on to the next story as is its calling.

11

On giving the order to shoot

Everyone was tired and in need of sleep. That included the hostages, police commanders, hospital staff, local and national news teams posted at the perimeter of the grounds, and the man waving the .357 Magnum.

A crisis with human lives on the line was approaching a breaking point. The clearly psychotic gunman became more desperate and demanding as the situation approached hour 31.

Nothing the hostages said — nothing police negotiators said or did — assuaged his anger and grief.

As each tidbit of information came his way, and as the now precious minutes ticked by, the Police Director knew time was running short. He needed a distraction, perhaps the use of a stun device. And he needed someone who knew how to shoot well and without hesitation.

******

During every police executive's tenure come the big cases — the ones that fill front pages and TV screens, sometimes for days on end, and are remembered years or decades later. I certainly had my share of those.

I spent time not long ago reviewing my own records and newspaper clippings. The hard part was culling the list of major events and cases that might be considered among the most sensational. They would include out-of-state killers hired to commit murders in our city, the execution of an undercover policeman, record-setting and multi-state drug captures, the

153

busting of organized crime syndicates, the finding of a kidnapped teenager and her abductor months later in a church attic. Or some of the more grievous police misconduct cases.

There's not enough ink or paper in one book to really list them all, but the first one that comes to mind was a day-long hostage situation that ended outside two high-rise buildings in east Memphis — Clark Tower and White Station Tower — late in the day on March 18, 1978.

It was a terrifying kidnapping and standoff that required critical decisions and could have left multiple people dead if things had gone badly.

An all-points bulletin had been issued in the Mid-South the day before for the arrest of a 38-year-old ex-convict named Howard Guess. He was wanted for armed robbery in Little Rock and in his hometown of Jacksonville, Arkansas. Jacksonville police had picked him up in connection with the robbery there but a witness couldn't positively identify him so he was released.

He made his way toward the Mississippi River and West Tennessee. In the car was Deborah Jean Allen, 24. Guess had abducted her earlier this day in a Little Rock parking lot. Police later determined he had drugged her as she was "half asleep most of the day."

The next sighting of Guess was near Somerville, Tennessee, when he walked into Sonny Boy's Grocery on U.S. 64 and demanded two candy bars and cash from the female store clerk whose husband owned the store. He raised his shirt and showed her his pistol.

Just then a man named Charles Branch walked into the store. Guess pointed his gun and ordered the man into a back room where he tied the man's hands and took money from his wallet.

Guess drove away with about $120 and the candy. At the store police were alerted. After Guess drove through Somerville and turned onto Tennessee Highway 76 toward Williston, pursuing police cars caught up with him and ran him off the road. Guess alighted, put a gun to his hostage's head and marched her to a nearby house. There he kicked in the door and ordered the man inside, Les Flannigan, to drive them away in Flannigan's yellow pickup truck.

Fugitive Guess now had two hostages. He made Flannigan drive to Moscow then turn south toward Rossville. There another officer was waiting and shot a tire on the pickup but didn't bring it to a stop. Guess and hostages turned around and soon forced off the road a silver-gray Ford LTD driven by Josephine Pugh. Also in the car was Pugh's four-year-old daughter Trinity.

Guess commandeered that car. As he did, Flannigan escaped. Now Guess had three hostages. He told Pugh to drive, moved Allen to the front passenger seat, and he sat in the back, holding the frightened girl in his lap.

The kidnapping next reached Collierville where police were able to bring the car to a stop. But officers backed away as Guess threatened his hostages. He demanded a car with a police radio. When police complied, that car moved toward Memphis where Sheriff Gene Barksdale and deputies were waiting and had put up blockades.

The next encounter happened at Shady Grove and Poplar Avenue in east Memphis where a roadblock had been set up. It was 2:25 p.m. A police dispatcher reported there was trouble inside the car. As officers took cover at several vantage points, Barksdale negotiated with Guess for about an hour, shouting pleas and warnings. Police closed Poplar Avenue and rerouted traffic.

Finally Guess agreed to relinquish a loaded shotgun on the floorboard but refused to hand over his 22-caliber pistol. He said he would give up the shotgun in return for a police escort to a location he wouldn't disclose. Barksdale arranged a two-car escort for the Ford. Barksdale was in a Sheriff's patrol car in front. Guess and his hostages were behind him, and a third car filled with Memphis police officials was in the rear.

The caravan moved a short distance to Poplar Avenue and I-240 but stopped. Guess said he was thinking about where he wanted to go. Minutes later he was ready and the parade drove west on Poplar, stopping once again a few minutes after 4 p.m. in the parking lot adjacent to Clark Tower and White Station Tower. It seemed that Guess was waiting for darkness to carry out whatever plan he had.

As the situation stalled, people began crowding along Poplar Avenue, rubbernecking. There weren't enough police cruisers to control the traffic. Some citizens drove to within 15 yards of the kidnap car and then parked not far away. Inside Clark Tower, office workers peered from windows. Over the next hour, Barksdale walked back and forth between the cars trying to talk Guess down. Barksdale, who thought Guess was popping a lot of pills, said each time he had to prove he wasn't carrying a weapon.

Once Guess pointed his gun at Barksdale's face and demanded money. He got another $27. He demanded money from the other officers in Barksdale's car. He collected another $7.

Around 5:30 Guess said he wanted to make a deal with a newspaper for money and to tell his story in his own words. *The Commercial Appeal* sent a reporter who spent nearly half an hour talking to Guess.

Karanja Ajanaku, who later led the *Tri-State Defender* staff, said everyone in the car was calm when he spoke with Guess. Editor Michael Grehl agreed to provide some money out of concern for the hostages but didn't promise a story. By that time there were an estimated 1,000 people watching. Some were drinking beer in their cars as they waited to see the outcome. By now there was plenty of police presence but no attempt was made to move people because of fear it would provoke Guess. Barksdale later said Guess apparently was enjoying the show.

At dusk the order was given to move people away. The parking lot was emptied except for a couple of cruising squad cars, and people inside the office towers were told to move away from the windows.

Guess had demanded he be allowed to leave and started threatening to shoot hostages. It was at this point I played a critical role. I had been at the scene most of the afternoon and decided we should offer him an escape by helicopter. When Barksdale told him, Guess liked the idea.

I then told my commanders to make sure we sent our Huey helicopter and — for God's sake — tell the pilot to turn off the motor when he landed in the parking lot between the buildings. The reason was simple: once a Huey is turned off it essentially is disabled without critical start-up gear.

I was not going to allow Guess to fly off in a helicopter with hostages. I sent word that good marksmen should be brought in and that if anyone had a clear shot at Guess when the little girl was clear — as he got to the copter or climbed in — that shot should be taken.

It was about 7:30 p.m. when the helicopter landed, nearly nightfall.

Things happened quickly. Guess came out with his hostages. He held the small girl in his arms and the gun to her head. Besides the pilot, there were four officers in the copter, one hiding. Guess ordered the three he could see out and told the girl's mother to search the men for weapons. They had handguns but she said they were unarmed.

Guess then spotted the fourth officer in the copter and ordered him out. Barksdale walked up as agreed and took the girl into his arms as Guess climbed into the helicopter. Barksdale turned away, shielding the girl, as the first shot rang out, followed by a flurry of more gunfire.

Guess was dead. Allen, who was seven months pregnant, was shot in both legs and an arm but her unborn child was not hurt. Two of the helicopter crewmen also were wounded.

A Memphis police sharpshooter had fired the first shot, which fatally wounded Guess, but the hostage-taker emptied his firearm rapidly at people standing outside the copter as he was dying. Other officers then returned his fire.

It was an easy decision for me to order the shooting.

Guess's mental condition was deteriorating, and if he was taking pills, that could make things worse. The ordeal had lasted for almost eight hours and I was concerned with the condition of the hostages as well as what Guess might end up doing as soon as he figured out the helicopter wasn't going anywhere. Often such situations come to an end with a hostage-taker killing a hostage and then shooting himself. As for the Huey: it took several bullets but was put back in service.

I will tell of another case that involved a home invasion and the killing of a police officer on duty. I include this one because it also ended with the kind of police misconduct I had been fighting to end for five years.

It was January 14, 1982. Three men flew into the airport from the west coast. They rented a car and then a room at a Holiday Inn on Shelby Oaks Lane. That night around 7:30 they drove to a home on Shady Grove Road.

At the front door they identified themselves as police officers then pushed their way in, tied up several family members and started ransacking the home for valuables and money. One family member was able to make a call for help.

The first officer to respond was Larry Childress. As soon as he got out of his squad car a gunfight erupted. Childress was hit and died in an ambulance ride to the hospital. The three men fled. Two were caught on foot by other responding police officers who had quickly covered the dense neighborhood. The third man got away in the rental car.

The captured suspects were identified as Gene Alfred Voss and Jimmy Dean Garrett. Both were from Los Angeles. Voss was identified as the shooter.

The victims were interviewed but the family declined to discuss the matter "on advice of their attorney." Although there was speculation the out-of-town trio was hired to collect some sort of debt, that was never proved or disproved.

A week later Voss was transported to the city hospital. He had complained of injuries suffered when he was arrested. A tactical unit officer drove. The jail officer rode in the front. A second tactical unit officer rode in back with Voss as extra security.

When Voss arrived at the hospital he had more injuries than when he left the jail. He bitterly complained that he had been beaten with a nightstick. The attending physician verified the fresh wounds, including a broken wrist.

The three officers were questioned. The one in the back seat denied assaulting Voss. The one driving said he hadn't seen or heard a thing. But the jailer told interviewers he heard "something going on, but I was too scared to look back."

The tactical unit officers who apparently believed they could with impunity take matters — the law — in their own hands and avenge the death of Childress were charged with assault and fired.

There are a lot of countries around the globe where law enforcement officers are allowed to abuse, even torture, prisoners. The United States of America isn't one. That never should be allowed in this country. Beating a restrained person, including a prisoner accused of murder of a cop, is plainly and simply against the law. How often it must be said: the role of a police officer is not to dispense punishment.

A second critical hostage situation on my watch unfolded at midday on Thursday, February 4, 1982. This too became a national story. Young Robert Goulet's grieving father blamed his ex-wife, a pediatrician and doctors and researchers at St. Jude Children's Research Hospital for the boy's death. A year before, after viewing a telethon about St. Jude and consulting with a doctor in Lima, Ohio, Phyllis Goulet had sought leukemia treatment for her son in Memphis at the hospital founded by Danny Thomas. After some improvement, the six-year-old child relapsed and died. Now a hostage crisis was starting just as St. Jude's 29th anniversary celebration was getting under way.

More than filled with grief, and armed with a powerful .357 magnum revolver and extra ammunition, Jean Claude Goulet of La Place, Louisiana, walked into the hospital and took four employees hostage. The ordeal would last for 32 tense hours and end in a dramatic life or death struggle.

Goulet quickly made threats to kill one of his hostages and demanded national television coverage to explain why he believed the research hospital and the boy's doctors were to blame for his son's death. He held at gunpoint a nurse, a leukemia researcher, a psychological examiner and a psychiatrist on the first floor of the psychiatry wing. Three hours into the crisis, Goulet let the psychiatrist go in exchange for burgers from the hospital's canteen.

The rest of that day and night and into the following day Goulet alternated between making verbal threats, waving his gun and having calm conversations with his hostages and police over a negotiating phone line we had established. The conversations ranged over various subjects as the hours passed — not just the death of his son. The room they were in was small and had no food, water or bathroom facilities. Goulet and his three hostages were packed in a room about eight feet by eight feet square.

As the negotiations continued, Goulet's demands to appear on ABC's *20/20* news show or on CBS's *60 Minutes* gave way to agreeing to allow the researcher hostage, Dr. Paul Bowman, to tape a long and rambling monologue of the man's views on leukemia to run on local radio stations. That plan went forward and five stations aired the statement live.

Goulet listened but decided what he was hearing wasn't authentic. He thought he might be listening to a CB radio output rather than FM radio. He demanded the stations air it again.

Station executives felt Goulet was escalating his demands. I agreed and asked them to stop live coverage. We knew this was risky but we were beginning to think that the only reasonable ending was to find a way to physically stop the man. We knew that probably meant we had to kill him.

Negotiations continued throughout the second day with little change except for one telling fact: Goulet kept cocking his gun. We could hear the clicking sound over the phone.

Later the hostages talked about how they believed he was a mentally ill individual and deeply depressed. They tried to soothe him with words. They complimented him. In the end it didn't make any difference.

As night came on the second day, we decided to act. I sent people into the air duct system that led to the room's ceiling. They sought a way to drop a stunning device into the room. Instead, the noise they made distracted Goulet. While we did this, we stationed four officers, including an assault marksman, at the door to prepare to storm the room.

The hostages sensed things were moving. They tried to position themselves where they might not be in the line of fire from the door. Bothered by the noise above, Goulet climbed onto a table to pry up ceiling tiles with his gun and to cram paper and other material into an air vent to stop the sounds. As Goulet stuffed the revolver in his pants pocket so that he could work at the vent with both hands, Bowman decided he had only that moment to act.

He lunged for Goulet's legs and the two men went tumbling off the table and onto the floor, the gun falling away. As Goulet grabbed for the gun, the two women ran toward the door screaming for help.

Three officers threw their bodies at the door and it burst open. Close behind them came Patrolman Jay Thurman, our best sharpshooter. He raised an M16 automatic rifle and fired a burst of four bullets that entered Goulet in a straight vertical line down his chest. He died instantly.

The only hostage injury was a dislocated shoulder. Dr. Bowman was knocked over by the officers who fell into the room

162

and then lurched sideways to give Thurman his open shot.

A sad and desperate act was over.

Afterwards the hostages said they were sure that killing Goulet was the only path that would get them out of the situation alive. They held a news conference in my office to describe the ordeal. Two talked and one added a comment here or there but mostly wept silently.

"There was no way to get out unless we were rescued," Dr. Bowman said. "He had a plan to die."

The St. Jude episode was an unfortunate and horrible circumstance — one where deadly force proved the only option available to brave law enforcers who had pledged to protect and serve. I was never more proud of the Memphis Police Department than I was on that day.

12

Recruiting the public's help

A politician, a philanthropist and a secretary walk into an office. Although that sounds like the first line of a tired joke, it describes the actual moment when the concept of a community-police partnership that Buddy Chapman longed for and believed in took distinct form.

Memphis groaned under the weight of unprecedented growth in serious crimes in the early 1980s. The litany would sound familiar to a Memphian living in the first quarter of the 21st Century: record numbers of homicides, aggravated assaults, thefts and rapes. Not for the first time the city had the title "murder capital" slung over its shoulders.

For Chapman, daily life was leaping out of the proverbial frying pan and into the flames one day and living it vice versa the next. Just as he was largely eliminating rampant wrong-doing from within the police department (and city jail) — just as he was finishing remolding the force into a better crime-fighting constabulary — barbarians of the criminal kind seemed to be pounding at the city's gates.

*****

We were caught between twin bullies. New data showed a dramatic rise in every category of felony crime while declining revenues caused a freeze on hiring new police officers.

In April 1981 the number of commissioned officers stood at 1,193 — far below the 1,600 men and women short-termed

164

Director Jay Hubbard had proposed for the department back in 1976. As I looked for ways to tighten the budget and do more with less, I also was losing on average three officers a month. Worse, the U.S. Comprehensive Employment and Training Act which was funding 30 of the 70 "detention specialists" in the city jail was ending in September.

I began drawing up plans to eliminate special units, such as Narcotics, Organized Crime, Aviation, Criminal Intelligence and the Tactical Squad. Those would be replaced in later years by cross-jurisdictional taskforces. I found it ironic that we had received praise from Main Justice for our organized crime unit and as a result we were guiding other big city police forces on setting up their own units to fight organized crime.

At least the jail personnel problem would be handled in two years' time when an agreement would be reached for city jail operations to merge with Shelby County's new internment facility.

As I pondered the seeming Gordian knot, Henry Evans, the chief administrative officer for the city of Memphis, announced his resignation. This was a blow to me personally. Not only was Henry a close friend and steadfast supporter of my reforming efforts, his advice always was right.

He and I had worked together since I was Mayor Chandler's executive assistant. I had learned that he had been essential in overcoming Chandler's doubts about appointing me police director. After his departure I missed his steady hand and wise counsel — rare qualities in any government bureaucracy — the rest of my tenure. The budget pressure forced me to sharpen my pencil and outline cuts.

I slimmed the Inspectional Services Bureau and the helicopter squad, folding officers into the detective and uniform ranks. The interstate highways patrol squad and the officers assigned to control downtown traffic and parking were folded into an expanded Traffic Investigation Squad. I decreased the ranks of Internal Affairs and instructed dispatchers not to send cars on non-emergency complaints within 30 minutes of shift change times.

I made a hard decision to cut 37 civilian employees across the department's divisions. All these steps to save money and use officers as best I could were the only means at my disposal to boost police effectiveness in the face of the surge in violent crime.

As the city grew more concerned about the growing crime problem, plain citizens and community leaders clamored for something to be done. I began sharing the hot seat with the Mayor and the city council.

When big problems loom, city and community leaders often gather forces and hold highly visible public meetings. This happened in May 1981 when hundreds of officials and leading citizens met over two days at the Cook Convention Center to establish what was labeled in the press a "three-pronged attack on crime." The strategy was to coordinate crime-fighting efforts among law enforcers, judges and corrections officials.

The conference drew state and federal officials. The FBI's Bob Hale described the effort as unique in Tennessee. Panel discussions would tackle all sides of the issue. The list of participants proved everybody was concerned or wanted to be seen as doing something. Attendees included U.S. Attorney Hickman Ewing, Assistant District Attorney John Fowlkes, U.S. Rep. Harold Ford, Shelby County Commission Chair Clair Vander Schaaf, U.S. Senator James Sasser, TBI director Arzo Carson, Judges James Beasley and Nancy Sorak, and many more. A final report would be sent to Tennessee's legislature for consideration.

Long-term solutions were hard to find, but the confab did serve to put a spotlight on a lot of issues, including the bail and parole policies, prison conditions and other parts of the criminal justice system. Newspaper stories and editorials kept the heat on officials across the city, county and state.

I seemed to be speaking to community groups nearly every night as the public's concern reached new levels. Not only was crime occurring more often, the perception was that crime was everywhere and all the time.

That included Whitehaven.

I was invited — it would be more accurate to say I was ordered — by the Whitehaven Community Association to come and face citizens at a community meeting there one night. The Mayor and City Councilman Ed McBrayer joined me. About 1,000 citizens were on hand. The crowd was upset by local crime but also worried about Chandler's proposed property tax increase to raise funds the legislature had declined to provide.

Taxes came up first. Chandler explained why the increase was necessary and the assembly mumbled angrily. McBrayer stood and said, "I will be trying to cut the budget. I cannot vote for a 70-cent tax increase." The crowd roared at that.

When it was my turn I stood and talked about the need to get tougher on the criminals. I knew that this would be met favorably.

"We're going to have to do some things to criminals so bad that they'll prefer not to undergo that type of treatment again," I said. The ovation was strong.

I have to say now that while I still believe in strong measures against those of the criminal class, I also know that punishment isn't the only answer. Yes, punishment should fit the crime and repeat offenders shouldn't be given their liberty too liberally. But at that time I was trying to formulate something more.

There had been a recent rape that particularly disturbed the neighborhood. Three young men had been charged with raping a woman and her young daughter. I explained the men hadn't planned the rape. They were out to steal a car. It was a carjacking.

"When they stole a car, it had two females in it and they said, 'Why not?' What we've got to give them is that 'why not,'" I said.

As I continued driving around the community to talk to more groups — neighborhood associations, churches, civic organizations — I worked on my message. I thought I was getting closer that night in Whitehaven. I declared that crime wasn't a police problem. I called it a societal problem. I began telling people that solving crime "rests with you." I said that when the whole community begins to work on crime, change will come.

I knew this was true. But the tactics were vague. I was trying to formulate how a community could begin to work hand-in-hand with law enforcement to make a difference.

One possible tactic walked into my office in the form of three people on June 11, 1981. It was a Thursday morning. I had no idea that something I was looking for was about to present itself, nor that it was something that would touch the rest of my life.

That morning my secretary ushered into the office two men I knew well, Bob James and P.K. Seidman.

James was a city councilman extraordinaire. He took deep dives into the city's budget every year. He knew all the line items, where the money was going and where there was a potential for waste. He also chaired the city council's Law Enforcement Committee.

Philip or P.K. Seidman was one of four brothers who had

established one of the world's leading accounting firms in New York City. He obtained a law degree at the Memphis Law School (later part of the University of Memphis) and settled here. Over time he began using his wealth to better the city and its institutions, becoming one of the city's leading philanthropists.

I greeted the pair, they sat down and I listened to a proposal.

Seidman and James had visited the city of Albuquerque, New Mexico, to learn about a unique program that city had started in 1978. It was called CrimeStoppers.

"We think we need something like it here," James said.

The program was showing real results in helping address crime.

"What can I do to help?" I asked.

They explained they wanted to establish the same program under the same name in Memphis. It would involve the start-up of a nonprofit entity with an independent citizens' board of directors whose purpose would be to raise funds for cash rewards to be paid to anonymous tipsters who would call in with information. The tips would be passed to police investigators.

The two men said they had money to get the program started but needed a location and staffing. As they talked, I could feel pieces of a puzzle coming together in my mind.

We had a former fire station that we were using for a police boxing gym at that time. It had office space in the rear. I called together members of my command staff to figure out how to create a small workforce quickly. We found some limited-duty police officers to help get the plan started and I volunteered a police sergeant, Tommy Tabor, to serve as a coordinator and liaison to the new agency.

Soon an organizational meeting was held at the Memphis Publishing Company building on Union Avenue, not far from downtown, and CrimeStoppers of Memphis and Shelby County was born. The enthusiasm was palpable. Everyone recognized that something important was getting under way.

In two months the new entity opened its doors and a phone line for business. Citizens were promised up to $1,000 for information that helped police make an arrest and charge. Conviction on a crime was not necessary.

The morning newspaper pledged to report stories about the new nonprofit and nonpartisan agency. Seidman agreed to chair the Board of Directors and James was the first vice chair. The agency's board began with 42 directors.

The citizen volunteers on the board of directors would select a crime to be featured each Monday on the front page of *The Commercial Appeal*. A billboard company in town promised several boards to promote CrimeStoppers and the cash awards to be offered to tipsters. Plans got underway to show re-enactments of crimes on local television newscasts.

The first featured crime was a series of fire bombings at five businesses, including three Big Star grocery stores, in Whitehaven in the early morning hours of August 21. Fire Department arson investigators were hampered by personnel shortages at that time and hadn't uncovered a single clue about the bombings.

It's hard now to describe the energy and enthusiasm that the creation of CrimeStoppers built in the city. Something tangible — a new tool for fighting crime — was available and provided a real sense of hope across the city. The newspaper's participation was critical to this wave of optimism. The coverage was consistent and it must be said that CrimeStoppers did supply the newspaper with good reading material.

I had no idea then that one day more than two decades later I would become the longest serving executive director of the agency I helped launch. But I did know immediately that CrimeStoppers gave me a real and practical way to tell people how the wider community — citizens who wanted to help or perhaps were in the know and just needed cash — could work with law enforcement to bring bad actors to justice.

A month after we began, the new CrimeStoppers had its first result. Two crooks had been burglarizing homes in St. Louis and carrying the stolen items to Memphis to sell to cronies here. They were fairly clever.

While in Memphis they committed more burglaries and transported those items back to St. Louis for sale there. Someone called in a tip identifying them. Detectives worked the case based on the information and made the arrests.

A second tip soon after broke up a similar crime. Two men let it be known on the streets that they had guns, furs, liquor and silver available from a big burglary in Horn Lake, Mississippi. They too were caught and $20,000 in stolen goods were recovered.

CrimeStoppers was off and running.

That same month the city was hit by a brutal sexual assault — one whose circumstances will seem all too familiar to contemporary Memphis readers.

A female jogger was attacked from behind as she ran. She was dragged into some wooded underbrush, struck with an iron bar, bound and gagged and raped. She managed to drag herself to the street where a public works crew saw her and called for help. A few days later, armed with information from a tipster, sex crimes detectives identified, located and arrested the man.

Unfortunately, the judge set the case for trial but released the accused individual on a low bond despite the objections of police and prosecutors. While the man was free he raped a second victim, bringing about a heavy public outcry. He was caught a second time and remained behind bars.

In the early months of 1982 I wasn't aware that the heady times of being considered a national expert on police reform were approaching an end. All the connections I made in the nation's capital — at the U.S. Justice Department and serving on the White House Advisory Council and the International Association of Police, most notably — led me to consult with other police agencies on ways to reorganize and reform practices. It was a busy travel year.

Our new CrimeStoppers program gave me more to share and it became a police-community model as I helped other communities start their own versions. I began to hone my message in Memphis and elsewhere about seeing the struggle against crime as a whole-community responsibility.

By now most people in the know assumed that Mayor Wyeth Chandler would not run for another term in office. It was well known that he wanted an appointment to a judgeship but he maintained his decision was dependent in part on who wanted to run for mayor. The election was two years away.

Two people had expressed interest. One was Richard (Dick) Hackett. He had been involved in Chandler's mayoral campaigns and had used those contacts to win election for Shelby County Court Clerk in 1978. The other interested party was Mike Cody, the former U.S. Attorney for West Tennessee.

Chandler, a Republican, preferred Hackett to Cody, whom he considered too liberal. There were rumors — mirrored by newspaper editorials and a political cartoon — that some sort of back-door agreement was in the works. Gov. Lamar Alexander would appoint Chandler as a judge, paving the way for an appointment of an interim mayor by the City Council. The players in the scheme seemed to be several City Council members and U.S. Rep. Harold Ford.

As schemes sometimes go, there were moving parts.

On Friday, September 10, 1982, Alexander announced his decision to name Chandler a judge. The Mayor, however, said his acceptance would be contingent on who was selected as his short-term successor.

The City's charter is clear. The council has 20 days to appoint someone. During that time of consideration, the council chairperson serves as the first interim mayor. If the council couldn't reach an agreement during the 20 days, the city chief administrative officer would serve until an election could be held.

The frontrunner for the interim job was Councilman Oscar Edmonds. He wasn't aligned with Chandler or Alexander but he had the backing of the city's Democrats. Even so, Chandler said Edmonds was acceptable to him. Alexander made the court appointment and J.O. Patterson, Council chair, became acting mayor for the next 20 days.

The council then tried to choose an interim appointment but could not reach an accord on Edmonds or anyone else, so Wallace Madewell, the city's CAO, became acting mayor.

In three weeks' time three different men sat in the mayor's office. Meanwhile, supporters of Dick Hackett filed a lawsuit challenging the provision of the replacement language. Their position was that two years was an unreasonable length of time for the city to go without a duly-elected mayor.

A judge agreed with that assessment and a special election was set in December. Immediately Cody and Hackett launched their mayoral campaigns. It was a hard-fought but short race. Hackett won.

Everyone in Chandler's administration had worked with Hackett in one way or another. No one expected him to fire all the directors of city divisions but that is exactly what he did. It especially came as a surprise because Chandler's well-organized political apparatus helped get him elected.

Hackett put out the message that any directors who had served in civil service positions previously could revert to those positions until their retirement date, or they could retire immediately. Everyone else had to go.

Since all of us directors were only a few months shy of qualifying for pension benefits, a group approached him to work out an arrangement that would help those so close to the benefits.

He refused to budge. I likened it to the French Revolution, with Hackett supporters roaming the hallways of government, looking for someone to cart off to the guillotines. Words to that effect happened to be my final quote to the press as Director of Police for the City of Memphis.[18]

Our duties were over. My reforms were done. We all collected personal effects and went off to contemplate "what's next" in our lives. For me, that meant at first working in the private sector. I found interesting jobs and new challenges in my next career. My wife and I enjoyed traveling and life was more simple. Then one day I got a phone call from a CrimeStoppers board member. Would I consider applying for the job of executive director?

---

[18] *Memphis Press-Scimitar*

Call me surprised, I thought.

And — yes — you still can call me Director.

Epilogue

Bringing systemic change to a large urban police department — whether today or half century ago — never is easy and cannot happen overnight.

Police agencies are naturally insular and in many ways isolated from the community. Without proper leaders who maintain a broad perspective and who can resist the temptation to be defensive, personnel often tend to see themselves as working and living apart from the public they serve. Without consistent and conspicuous discipline in the ranks, and a full consciousness of the possible negative results of the isolation, problems will fester and grow.

This pattern has emerged more than once since the 1970s.

Whenever problems do arise, immediate solutions are demanded from the outside. The usual call today is for a vague concept of police "reform" (if not defunding or even abolishment). By any name — change, reform, reorganization — departmental renewal is something that must involve the full community's voice, and only occurs when strong police and political leadership exists.

Buddy Chapman played the role of a reformer when he was in charge of the Memphis Police Department because he understood that fundamental changes were needed in the force, from the elimination of brutality to the banning of racial discrimination and corruption.

But he didn't act alone. He moved with the help of court orders, community activism, new enlightenment within the police ranks, creative solutions found in other big city departments, encouragement from friends and associates, and the slow but steady support of the Mayor.

Slow and steady has never been Chapman's natural style.

All his life he was raised and trained to "see a problem, find a fix." He has never been one for putting off until later something begging to be done today. Yet he also learned that the big items require patience and a certain steadfast determination.

Good police work must take place in an ever-changing world, where cultural norms evolve, and policies need to change to meet new challenges.

And yet, the ageless challengers to law enforcement— the lawbreakers —persist. Indeed, human history shows the criminal class always will be among us.

Two years into Buddy Chapman's tenure as police director, felony crimes had risen across the board — assaults, robberies and thefts, rapes and murders. At the time this book is being finished, the same report has been issued to the community: all major crimes have seen an increase over the previous year.

To help break cycles of violence and lawlessness, several things are required of a police force —they were true decades ago, are true today, will be so 50 years from now.

First and foremost, a police force must see its work as a partnership with the community, and the public must see it that way as well. Neither should see the other as the enemy.

Second, police officers must follow the law and regulations at all times. Those who do not must be removed from the ranks. Those who take the law into their own hands must be terminated and punished under the law.

Third, police leadership must require that laws and policies be followed and must demand discipline from top to bottom. Bad police operatives cannot thrive when a responsible command structure is in control at all times.

Fourth, police leaders must be visible and accessible to the rank and file officers, as well as to the public.

A police force, no matter its size, cannot reduce crime on its own.

It is too easy to think that adding more police or new technologies will reduce crimes statistics. While these can help, crime only subsides when a community refuses to accept lawlessness as a normal occurrence or something that can't be stopped.

Across the nation today, gun crime is on the rise, as are calls to do something about the problem. There are signs that local and state governments are beginning to act in the face of public demands for action — from so-called "red-flag" laws, to destroying confiscated weapons, to even new bans on military-grade assault rifles.

Whether this is a trend — or whether America's gun culture will resist new laws and regulations remains an open question as this book goes to press.

Never uncertain is this truism: a police department is most effective when it is working with — indeed intricately part of — the community it serves.

THE END

www.ingramcontent.com/pod-product-compliance
Lightning Source LLC
Chambersburg PA
CBHW030255130626
46549CB00002B/542

9 7 9 8 9 8 9 3 6 4 4 0 4